complete

cooking

complete
cooking

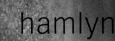

hamlyn

This edition first published in the U.K. in 1997 by
Hamlyn, a division of Octopus Publishing Group Limited
2–4 Heron Quays, London E14 4JP

Reprinted 2001

Printed in Hong Kong

ISBN 0 600 60608 2

NOTES

Both metric and imperial measurements have been given in all
recipes. Use one set of measurements only, and not a mixture of
both.

Standard level spoon measurements are used in all recipes.
1 tablespoon = one 15 ml spoon
1 teaspoon = one 5 ml spoon

Eggs should be medium to large unless otherwise stated.
The Department of Health advises that eggs should not be
consumed raw. This book contains dishes made with raw or
lightly cooked eggs. It is prudent for more vulnerable people such
as pregnant and nursing mothers, invalids, the elderly, babies and
young children to avoid uncooked or lightly cooked dishes made
with eggs. Once prepared, these dishes should be kept refrigerated
and used promptly.

Meat and poultry should be cooked thoroughly. To test if poultry
is cooked, pierce the flesh through the thickest part with a skewer
or fork — the juices should run clear, never pink or red. Do not
re-freeze poultry that has been frozen previously and thawed.
Do not re-freeze a cooked dish that has been frozen previously.

Milk should be full fat unless otherwise stated.

Nut and Nut Derivatives

This book includes dishes made with nuts and nut derivatives. It
is advisable for customers with known allergic reactions to nuts
and nut derivatives and those who may be potentially vulnerable
to these allergies, such as pregnant and nursing mothers, invalids,
the elderly, babies and children to avoid dishes made with nuts
and nut oils. It is also prudent to check the labels of pre-prepared
ingredients for the possible inclusion of nut derivatives.

Pepper should be freshly ground black pepper unless otherwise
stated.

Fresh herbs should be used, unless otherwise stated. If
unavailable, use dried herbs as an alternative, but halve the
quantities stated.

Measurements for canned food have been given as a standard
metric equivalent.

Ovens should be pre-heated to the specified temperature — if
using a fan-assisted oven, follow the manufacturer's instructions
for adjusting the time and the temperature.

Vegetarians should look for the 'V' symbol on a cheese to ensure it
is made with vegetarian rennet. There are vegetarian forms of
Parmesan, feta, Cheddar, Cheshire, Red Leicester, dolcelatte and
many goats' cheeses, among others.

Contents

Utensils

Pizza slice

Stainless steel steamer

Pizza cutter

Colander

Olive oil canister

Garlic press

Measuring spoons   *Wooden spatula*

Mezzaluna

Stainless steel steamer
This is excellent for maintaining the texture and flavour of the finished dish.

Garlic press
A garlic press forces the garlic through a series of tiny holes. This also releases the oils so that the food

benefits from the full flavour of the clove.

Pizza/pasta cutter
This is used for cutting pizzas or pasta. Ensure that the wheel turns freely.

Pizza slice
This is a wide-bladed slice used to help lift and transfer

a pizza from the baking sheet to the plate. It is usually made of stainless steel.

Colander
This is basically a container with holes in, used for separating liquids and solids and for draining and rinsing food. It is usually made of plastic or stainless steel.

Measuring spoons
These come in sets with a tablespoon, a teaspoon, a half teaspoon, and a quarter teaspoon. They come in aluminium, plastic or stainless steel and measure both dry goods and liquids.

Spatula
Usually made of plastic, a

spatula has a wide, blunt blade. It is used for moving food around a bowl and for scraping round the edges of a mixing bowl.

Oil canister
This has a long thin spout which is useful for distributing oil evenly over salads and pans.

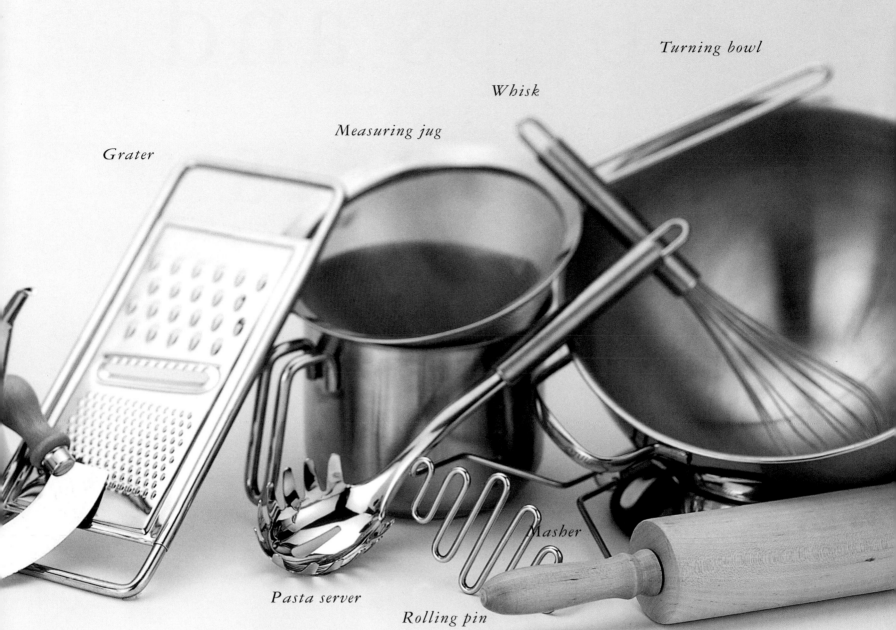

Grater

Measuring jug

Whisk

Turning bowl

Pasta server

Rolling pin

Masher

Mezzaluna

This uses a two-handled rocking motion to chop herbs and vegetables finely.

Grater

Graters come in a box shape or a single flat sheet. They have perforations which perform different functions. The fine holes are for grating spices and rind, the medium and large holes are for grating cheese and vegetables. They are usually made of stainless steel.

Measuring jug

This is a standardized liquid measure, with a pouring lip. It is usually marked in both metric and imperial. It is available in glass, plastic or stainless steel.

Pasta server

This is a long-handled stainless steel spoon, which is used for transferring pasta from the pan. It has teeth that pick up the pasta easily and a hole which allows the liquid to drain away.

Masher

A masher is used for mashing cooked, starchy vegetables such as potatoes or swede.

Rolling pin

This is used for rolling out pasta, pastry and bread dough. It should be heavy so that it does the work, not you. It can be made of wood, plastic, nylon or marble.

Turning bowl

This has a built-in stand to support it and to prevent it slipping. It enables ease of mixing, beating or folding at different angles. The stainless steel surface is hard wearing and easy to clean.

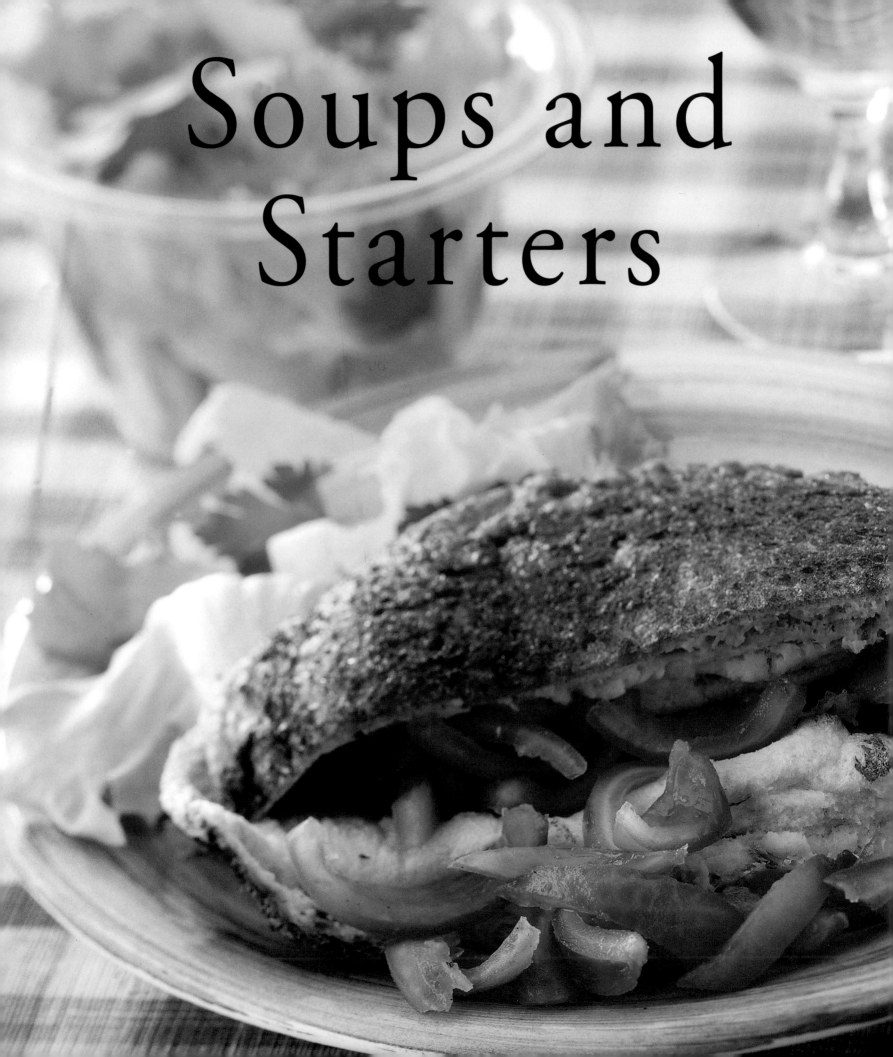

Soups and Starters

Bacon and Turnip Soup

25 g/1 oz butter or margarine
125 g/4 oz rindless smoked bacon, coarsely chopped
1 onion, chopped
375 g/12 oz potatoes, peeled and chopped
750 g/1½ lb turnips, peeled and chopped
1.2 litres/2 pints Chicken Stock (see page 10)
1 bay leaf
1 small sprig fresh thyme or ¼ teaspoon dried thyme
150 ml/¼ pint milk
salt and freshly ground black pepper
1 tablespoon finely chopped parsley to garnish (optional)

melt the butter or margarine in a heavy-based saucepan, add the bacon and cook over a moderate heat until crisp and golden. Remove the bacon with a slotted spoon and set aside.

cook the onion, potatoes and turnips in the bacon fat for about 5 minutes over a low heat. Add the stock, bay leaf and thyme.

bring to the boil then lower the heat and cook for 30–35 minutes or until all the vegetables are soft. Remove and discard the bay leaf and sprig of thyme, if used.

purée the mixture in a blender or food processor in batches until smooth. Transfer each successive batch to a clean saucepan. Add the reserved bacon and the milk, and season with salt and pepper if necessary.

cook over a moderate heat for 35 minutes or until the soup is hot but not boiling. Stir frequently.

serve at once in heated soup plates or bowls, and sprinkle each portion with a little finely chopped parsley, if liked.

Serves 6
Preparation time: *40–45 minutes*
Cooking time: *1½ hours*

Prawn Gumbo

This Cajun soup is native to the Louisiana coast of the USA. It can be made with a variety of vegetables, meats, and seafood, but okra is its most important ingredient, as it thickens the soup and provides a luxuriously rich texture.

50 g/2 oz long-grain white rice
50 g/2 oz butter
2 garlic cloves, crushed
I onion, chopped
I red pepper, cored, deseeded and finely chopped
4 ripe tomatoes, skinned and chopped
¼ teaspoon cayenne pepper or more to taste
1.2 litres/2 pints Fish Stock (see page 10)
375 g/12 oz okra (vegetable), trimmed and sliced
375 g/12 oz prawns, cooked and peeled, thawed if frozen and dried on absorbent kitchen paper
I tablespoon lime juice, freshly squeezed
salt and freshly ground black pepper

bring a large saucepan of lightly salted water to the boil. Add the rice and cook for 8–10 minutes or until tender. Drain the rice and set aside.

melt the butter in a large heavy-bottomed saucepan. Add the garlic and onion and cook gently for about 5 minutes or until soft and slightly golden. Add the red pepper and continue cooking over a moderate heat for a further 5 minutes, stirring constantly.

stir in the tomatoes and cayenne and mix well. Pour in the fish stock and bring the mixture to the boil. Add the okra, lower the heat, cover the pan and cook for 20 minutes, stirring occasionally.

add the prawns, rice and lime juice to the soup. Stir well, cover and simmer for a further 5–8 minutes. Season with salt and pepper and add a little more cayenne, if liked.

Serves 4–6
Preparation time: *20 minutes*
Cooking time: *50 minutes*

clipboard: Many recipes require skinned tomatoes – the method of skinning them is simple. Place the tomatoes in a bowl and pour over enough boiling water to cover. Leave for 1–2 minutes, then drain, cut a cross at the stem end of each tomato, and peel off the skins.

Mussel Chowder

The term 'chowder' originates from the New England seaboard of the USA. There are many recipes, but this retains the classic flavour.

2 tablespoons olive oil
250 g/8 oz streaky bacon, chopped
2 onions, finely chopped
I celery stick, finely sliced
I green pepper, cored, deseeded and finely chopped
450 ml/¾ pint Fish Stock (see page 10)
250 g/8 oz potatoes, peeled and diced
I bay leaf
½ teaspoon fresh marjoram leaves, chopped, or
¼ teaspoon dried marjoram
3 tablespoons plain white flour
300 ml/½ pint milk
500 g/1 lb mussels, cooked and shelled,
thawed if frozen
150 ml/¼ pint single cream
salt and white pepper
I tablespoon finely chopped parsley, to garnish

heat the olive oil in a heavy-based saucepan and cook the bacon, uncovered, over a moderate heat until browned. Add the onions, celery and pepper and cook for 5 minutes or until the vegetables soften. Stir frequently. Add the fish stock, potatoes, bay leaf and marjoram.

bring to the boil, then lower the heat, cover the pan and simmer for 15–20 minutes or until the potatoes are tender.

blend the flour with 150 ml/¼ pint of the milk in a small bowl. Whisk the mixture into the chowder, stir until it begins to boil then slowly add the remaining milk. Add salt and pepper to taste.

lower the heat, add the mussels and simmer gently for 5 minutes, stirring from time to time. Do not allow the chowder to boil. Stir in the cream and pour the chowder into a heated soup tureen. Sprinkle the parsley over the top to garnish and serve with crusty French bread.

Serves 4–6
Preparation time: *10–15 minutes*
Cooking time: *about 30 minutes*

clipboard: Mussels are delicious but they need very careful preparation if they are to be safe. Always buy them from a reputable fishmonger. Scrub them under plenty of cold running water. Carefully remove the beards. Discard any that open at this stage. Cook in plenty of boiling water and discard any that don't open when cooked. Use the small, plump European mussels for this recipe – the large New Zealand mussels are not suitable.

Fisherman's Soup
with a hot rouille

Rouille is a piquant sauce made from an aromatic combination of garlic and pimientos. It is traditionally spread on toasted bread and served with fish soup.

1 leek, chopped

2 onions, chopped

2 garlic cloves, crushed

5 tablespoons olive oil

3 tomatoes, skinned (see page 20) and chopped

2 potatoes, peeled and diced

1 large red snapper or 2 medium red mullets, scaled and cleaned

1 monkfish tail, skinned and filleted with the bone

750 ml/1¼ pints water

600 ml/1 pint dry white wine

2 strips orange peel

1 bay leaf

few sprigs of fresh fennel or thyme

½ teaspoon saffron strands (optional)

2 tablespoons chopped parsley

a little Fish Stock (see page 10) (optional)

salt and freshly ground black pepper

To garnish
French bread stick (baguette), sliced

1 x quantity of Rouille (see page 8)

4 tablespoons grated Gruyère cheese

sauté the leek, onions and garlic in the olive oil until soft and golden. Add the tomatoes and potatoes and cook gently for 2–3 minutes.

remove the head of the snapper or mullets and add to the pan with the monkfish bone. Add the water, wine, orange peel, herbs and seasoning and bring to the boil. Reduce the heat, add the fish, chopped into larger pieces and simmer gently for 15 minutes.

crush the saffron, if using between your fingers and add to the pan. Stir well and continue cooking gently for 15–20 minutes. Remove and discard the fish head, fish bones, bay leaf, orange rind and herb sprigs.

pour the soup into a liquidizer or blender and blend until smooth. Return to the pan and heat through gently. Add the parsley and, if it is too thick, you can thin it down with some fish stock.

toast the slices of French bread lightly on both sides, spread with the *rouille*, sprinkle with Gruyère and serve with the hot soup.

Serves 6–8
Preparation time: *15 minutes*
Cooking time: *50–55 minutes*

French Onion Soup

Onion soup is supposed to have originated in Les Halles, the Parisian food market. In fact, most countries have their own version of this heartwarming, juicy and fragrant soup.

50 g/2 oz butter
750 g/1½ lb onions, thinly sliced
2 teaspoons sugar
2 teaspoons plain flour
1 litre/1¾ pints Beef Stock (see page 10)
½ French bread stick (baguette), sliced
50 g/2 oz Gruyère cheese, grated
salt and freshly ground black pepper

melt the butter in a large saucepan and add the onions and sugar. Lower the heat to a bare simmer and cook the onions very slowly for 20–30 minutes until they are soft and a really deep golden brown. Stir occasionally and cook to a good colour without burning.

stir the flour into the onion mixture and cook over a very low heat for about 5 minutes, stirring well to prevent it burning or sticking to the bottom of the pan.

add the beef stock and the salt and freshly ground black pepper. Turn up the heat and bring to the boil, stirring all the time. Reduce the heat and simmer for 15–20 minutes. Taste the soup and add more salt and freshly ground black pepper if necessary.

toast the slices of French bread lightly on both sides in the meantime. Sprinkle with the grated Gruyère. Pour the soup into a hot tureen. Place a piece of toast in each serving bowl and ladle the hot soup over the top.

Serves 4–5
Preparation time: *15 minutes*
Cooking time: *1 hour*

Savoury Soufflé Omelette

This is a starter with a difference, as it is a delicious hybrid of omelette and soufflé. Vary the flavour by using a choice of tasty fillings.

Omelette

4 eggs
water
25–50 g/1–2 oz butter
salt and freshly ground black pepper

Savoury Fillings
Cheese

3 tablespoons grated Cheddar cheese

Fish

3 tablespoons flaked shellfish, white or smoked fish, in a Béchamel Sauce (see page 8)

Meat

3 tablespoons finely diced cooked chicken, *or*
3 tablespoons finely diced ham, *or*
3 tablespoons chopped crisp bacon

Vegetables

3 tablespoons cooked mixed vegetables, in a Béchamel Sauce (see page 8)

heat the grill on a medium setting before preparing the omelette.

separate the eggs and beat the yolks with the seasoning. Add about ½ teaspoon water. Heat the butter in a large frying pan.

whisk the egg whites until they stand in peaks and fold into the yolks just before cooking.

pour the eggs into the pan and cook until set on the bottom. Place the pan under the grill (take care the handle does not get too hot). Cook until the omelette is set.

cut the omelette lightly through the centre to make it easier to fold and add the filling of your choice. Fold away from the handle and tip on to a heated plate.

Serves 2
Preparation time: *5 minutes, plus filling*
Cooking time: *4–5 minutes*

Pâté de Campagne

This is one of an infinite variety of country pâté recipes found all over France. Each region has its speciality, handed down over generations. This version is moist, tender and deliciously flavoured.

50 g/2 oz butter, plus a little extra for greasing
2 onions, finely chopped
4 garlic cloves, crushed
500 g/1 lb pig's liver, diced
275 g/9 oz rindless streaky bacon rashers
500 g/1 lb lean pork, minced or chopped
2 tablespoons chopped parsley
½ teaspoon dried sage
¼ teaspoon ground mace
¼ teaspoon ground nutmeg
2 egg whites
2 tablespoons brandy
2 bay leaves
salt and freshly ground black pepper

grease a 500 g/1 lb terrine or loaf tin lightly.

melt the butter in a frying pan and sauté the onions and garlic gently for a few minutes until tender and golden. Transfer to a large bowl. Add the liver to the pan and fry until lightly browned. Remove and mince or chop.

chop 200 g/7 oz of the streaky bacon and add to the bowl with the liver, pork, parsley, sage, mace, nutmeg, salt and pepper, egg whites and brandy. Mix together well until thoroughly combined.

line the terrine or loaf tin with the remaining bacon rashers so that they hang over the sides. Fill with the pâté mixture and fold the bacon over the top. Put the 2 bay leaves on top and place in a roasting pan of hot water.

cook in a preheated oven, 190°C/375°F/Gas Mark 5, for 1½ hours or until the juices run clear and the pâté has shrunk from the sides of the tin.

leave the pâté to cool for 30 minutes then cover with a piece of greaseproof paper or kitchen foil and weigh it down with some light weights. Leave until completely cold and set. If you like, you can replace the bay leaves with fresh ones. Cover and refrigerate for about 36 hours. Serve sliced with toast or crusty bread.

Serves 8
Preparation time: *30 minutes*
Cooking time: *1½ hours*
Oven temperature: *190°C/375°F/Gas Mark 5*

Pot-Roast of Beef

4 tablespoons vegetable oil
25 g/1 oz butter
1.25–1.5 kg/2½–3 lb topside or silverside of beef
2 large onions, quartered
2 large carrots, peeled and cut into 1 cm/½ inch slices
1 bouquet garni or 2 sprigs each thyme, parsley and marjoram
4 black peppercorns
½ teaspoon salt
150 ml/¼ pint red wine mixed with 450 ml/¾ pint water
2 teaspoons cornflour

heat the oil and butter in a flameproof casserole, add the beef and turn until browned.

reduce the heat and pack the vegetables all round the beef. Add the herbs, peppercorns and salt. Pour in the wine and water.

cover the casserole closely with foil, then the lid and cook in a preheated oven, 150°C/300°F/Gas Mark 2, for 3 hours until the beef is tender and cooked through.

transfer the beef to a heated serving dish. Discard the herbs. Lift out the vegetables with a perforated spoon and place round the beef. Keep hot while making the sauce.

bring the cooking liquid in the casserole to the boil. Mix the cornflour with a little water to make a smooth paste, pour a little of the boiling gravy on to it, stirring well and pour back into the boiling gravy in the casserole, stirring constantly. If the sauce is too thick, thin with a little stock or water and return to the boil. Pour the sauce over the beef and vegetables and serve.

Serves 6
Preparation time: *30 minutes*
Cooking time: *3 hours 20 minutes*
Oven temperature: *150°C/300°F/Gas Mark 2*

clipboard: Economical joints of beef such as topside, silverside or brisket are ideal for this slow, gentle method of pot-roasting, which breaks down the tough fibres, and results in a tender, succulent, well-flavoured joint. In fact the meat is being cooked in the steam from the liquid ingredients, rather than roasted in the conventional manner.

Braised Beef
with cheese dumplings

25 g/1 oz beef dripping or oil
2 onions, sliced
750 g/1½ lb stewing beef, cubed
1 rounded tablespoon plain flour
1 teaspoon brown sugar
1 pinch of cinnamon
300 ml/½ pint brown ale
salt and freshly ground black pepper

Dumplings
125g/4 oz self-raising flour
50 g/2 oz suet, shredded, or margarine, melted
25 g/1 oz Cheddar cheese, grated
2–3 tablespoons water
salt and freshly ground black pepper

heat the fat or oil in a frying pan, cook the onions until soft, then transfer into a casserole. Brown the beef quickly on all sides in the pan, then add the flour and let it cook for 1 minute, stirring from time to time.

add the sugar and cinnamon and gradually pour in the brown ale. Stir well, then add salt and pepper to taste.

put the meat and gravy into the casserole, cover, and cook in a preheated oven, 180°C/350°F/Gas Mark 4 for 30 minutes. Then reduce the oven temperature to 160°C/325°F/Gas Mark 3, and continue cooking for 1 further hour.

make the dumplings next. Mix the dry ingredients together, season and add the water gradually. Add a little more if needed to make a fairly slack dough. Flour the hands and break the dough into 8 small pieces, then roll into little balls with the palms of the hands. Chill until required.

test the meat with a fork after 1½ hours cooking time. If necessary, cook for a further 30 minutes. If the casserole is dry, add some water or beer.

place the dumplings on top of the casserole about 20 minutes before the meat is ready, leave off the lid and cook until they are risen, about 20–30 minutes. Alternatively, poach the dumplings about 4 at a time in a saucepan of boiling salted water for about 15 minutes. Drain well.

Serves 4–6
Preparation time: *30 minutes*
Cooking time: *about 2 hours*
Oven temperature: *180°C/350°F/Gas Mark 4,* then *160°C/325°F/GasMark 3*

Beef Stroganoff

*This is still one of the most popular 'special occasion'
dishes, and requires good quality, tender meat.
This makes a delicious sauce with the sour cream
stirred into the meat juices.*

3 onions, finely chopped
50 g/2 oz butter
250 g/8 oz button mushrooms, thinly sliced
1 green pepper, deseeded and cut in fine strips
500g/1 lb fillet or good rump steak, cut into
strips 5cm/2 in long, 5 mm/¼ inch thick
150 ml/¼ pint double dairy soured cream
salt and freshly ground pepper
1 teaspoon chopped parsley, to garnish

fry the onions in half the butter in a large deep frying pan until pale
gold. Add the mushrooms and green pepper to the pan and cook for 5
minutes. Remove the onions, mushrooms and green pepper from the pan.

melt the remaining butter and heat, then fry the meat for about 4
minutes, turning it so it becomes evenly cooked.

return the onions, mushrooms and peppers to the pan, season well, stir
in the soured cream and blend well. Heat until piping hot but do not
allow to boil. Garnish with chopped parsley.

Serves 4
Preparation time: *10 minutes*
Cooking time: *15 minutes*

clipboard: A rather more economical version of this dish can be made
by using a cheaper cut of meat such as braising steak. Cut the meat into
strips as above, and marinate it in lemon juice overnight to tenderize it.

Lamb Casserole
with red wine and herbs

1.25kg/2½ lb shoulder of lamb (trimmed weight), boned and cubed

1 large onion, finely chopped

2 garlic cloves, crushed

2 large tomatoes, skinned (see page 20), deseeded and quartered

1 *bouquet garni* including thyme, parsley, rosemary, marjoram and bayleaf

rind of 1 orange, cut into thin strips

1 bottle of dry red wine

2 tablespoons olive oil

250 g/8 oz rindless streaky bacon, diced

300 ml/½ pint Chicken Stock (see page 10)

250 g/8 oz plain flour

salt and freshly ground black pepper

75 g/3 oz small black olives, to serve

1 tablespoon chopped parsley, to garnish

trim any excess fat from the cubed lamb. Put the meat in a large casserole dish with the onion, garlic, tomatoes, *bouquet garni*, orange rind, salt and 1 teaspoon pepper. Pour the wine over the top, add the oil and stir well. Cover and leave to marinate in the refrigerator for 4 hours.

blanch the bacon in boiling water for 2 minutes and drain. Add to the casserole with the chicken stock so that the lamb is well covered with liquid. Season with a pinch of salt.

mix the flour with a little water to form a paste, then roll into a thin strip. Press the paste between the casserole dish and lid to form a seal.

cook in a preheated oven, 200°C/400°F/Gas Mark 6, for 1 hour, then reduce the temperature to 180°C/350°F/Gas Mark 4 and cook for a further 2 hours. Discard the strip of flour paste and remove the *bouquet garni*.

sprinkle the casserole with black olives and garnish with parsley. Serve with plain boiled rice.

Serves 4–6
Preparation time: *15 minutes, plus 4 hours marinating*
Cooking time: *3 hours*
Oven temperature: *200°C/400°F/Gas Mark 6,* then *180°C/350°F/Gas Mark 4*

Rack of Lamb

2 lean best ends of neck of lamb, chined
750g/1½ lb courgettes
1 x 200 g/7 oz can sweetcorn, drained
75 g/3 oz fresh wholemeal breadcrumbs
rind, finely grated, and juice of 1 small orange
4 tablespoons Quark cheese or skimmed
milk soft cheese
375 g/12 oz baby sweetcorn cobs
1 tablespoon soya or sunflower oil
salt and freshly ground black pepper
rosemary sprigs, to garnish

remove the skin and most of the fat from the surface of the meat, leaving just a thin, even layer of fat. Cut away the meat from the top 3.5 cm/1½ inches of the rib ends and scrape them well. Using a sharp knife, score the surface of the fat in a diamond pattern.

grate 250 g/8 oz of the courgettes by hand or in a food processor and mix with the sweetcorn, breadcrumbs, orange rind and Quark or skimmed milk soft cheese. Season the mixture with salt and pepper.

shape the mixture into a long roll and place this along the curve of the bones of one joint; place the other joint over the first so that the bones interlock, forming 'crossed swords'. Tie them firmly with string and wrap the tops of the bones with aluminium foil to prevent them burning.

place the joint on a rack in a roasting tin. Place in a preheated oven, 180°C/350°F/Gas Mark 4, and cook for 1¼ hours until the lamb is just tender and still slightly pink in the centre.

cut the remaining courgettes into long sticks about the size of the baby corn cobs in the meantime. Place the courgettes and corn cobs in a pan with the oil and the orange juice. Sprinkle them with pepper and cover the pan tightly. Cook over a fairly high heat, shaking the pan occasionally until the vegetables are just tender.

remove the meat from the oven and skim any fat from the juices. Place the meat in the centre of a warmed platter and arrange the vegetables around it. Garnish with sprigs of rosemary. Mix the cooking juices and serve separately as a sauce.

Serves 6
Preparation time: *40–50 minutes*
Cooking time: *1¼ hours*
Oven temperature: *180°C/350°F/Gas Mark 4*

Flour, Grains and Rice

Popcorn

Couscous

Buckwheat flour

Pinhead oatmeal

Cornflour

Rye flakes

Popcorn
This is the dried kernels of sweetcorn which, when heated in oil, pop to form a fluffy corn snack. It can be coated with sugar or salt.

Buckwheat flour
This flour is made from roasted buckwheat seeds and is used in pancakes, blinis, crisp thin cakes and Asian soya noodles. The seeds came originally from central Asia, but the buckwheat plant is, in fact, a native of the Soviet Union.

Cornflour
A fine white flour, this is sometimes known as corn starch. It is made from corn kernels and is used in cooking to thicken sauces, gravies and puddings, and to make blancmange.

Rye flakes
Also known as rolled rye, rye flakes are cultivated to make flour and for distilling into whisky. They are also used in soups and casseroles.

Couscous
A pasta made from durum wheat and semolina, this is a staple in North African cooking. To cook couscous, soak it in boiling water, fluff it up with a fork and add a knob of butter or a little oil. Couscous is a good accompaniment to meat, fish and vegetable dishes.

Pinhead oatmeal
Also referred to as fine oatmeal, this has been finely ground so that it can be used in pancakes, oatcakes and muffins.

Wild rice
This is not, in fact, rice but the seeds of an aquatic grass that is native to the

Basmati rice

Soya flour

Plain flour

Wholemeal flour

Wild rice

Polenta

Minnesota Lakes in the US. It is surrounded by a tough husk which is long and dark brown and, when the husk is cooked, it bursts open to reveal a pale interior that can be boiled or steamed. Wild rice has a distinctive earthy flavour and is served as an accompaniment to fish, poultry or vegetables.

Basmati rice

A rice native to Asia, this is widely associated with Indian cuisine. Basmati rice should always be soaked before cooking.

Polenta

A thick porridge of cornmeal, water and butter, polenta can be eaten hot with Parmesan as a vegetarian dish, or it can be served either with chopped meat or with a sauce.

Soya flour

This is made from ground, roasted soya beans. It is rich in protein and carbohydrates. The bread made from it is rather sweet.

Wholemeal flour

This is a coarse-textured flour which can be used to make bread, cakes, biscuits and pasta. The flour is made by grinding the wheat kernel which includes the bran, the germ, and the endosperm. Wholemeal flour is particularly popular with health-conscious

eaters, because of its high fibre content.

Plain flour

After the flour has been ground, the germ and bran are removed, and the flour is bleached to remove the colour. White flour is used in the great majority of baking recipes.

flour, grains and rice   **57**

Catalan Pork Stew
with tomatoes and aubergines

150 ml/¼ pint olive oil
750g/1½ lb lean pork cut into 2.5 cm/1 inch cubes
1 large onion, sliced
2 garlic cloves, crushed
500 g/1 lb tomatoes, skinned (see page 20)
and chopped
1 green pepper, deseeded and chopped
1½ teaspoons paprika
150 ml/¼ pint Chicken Stock (see page 10)
1 aubergine, sliced
2–3 tablespoons seasoned flour
salt and freshly ground black pepper
1 tablespoon chopped coriander leaves, to garnish

heat 2 tablespoons of the oil in a large saucepan or flameproof casserole, add the pork and sauté gently until golden brown on all sides, turning occasionally. Remove from the pan with a slotted spoon.

add the onion and garlic and cook until soft and golden. Return the meat to the pan and stir in the tomatoes, green pepper, paprika and stock. Season with salt and freshly ground black pepper.

bring to the boil, cover with greaseproof paper and a lid and simmer gently for 1 hour or until the meat is tender.

dip the aubergine slices in seasoned flour. Heat some of the remaining oil in a large frying pan. When it is hot, fry the aubergine slices, a few at a time, until they are golden brown on both sides. Add more oil as required.

remove with a slotted spoon and pat dry with kitchen paper. Serve with the fried aubergine, scattered with coriander, and plain boiled rice.

Serves 4
Preparation time: *20 minutes*
Cooking time: *1¼ hours*

clipboard: If you dislike the slightly bitter taste of aubergines and wish to remove it, you can prepare them as follows. Sprinkle the slices with salt and leave for 20–30 minutes. Drain, rinse in cold water and dry on kitchen paper. They are now ready to use.

Stir-Fried Beef

with baby corn and red peppers

1 tablespoon Szechuan pepper

3 tablespoons vegetable oil

500 g/1 lb rump or fillet steak, cut into
thin strips across the grain

2 fresh green chillies, deseeded and finely chopped

1 onion, thinly sliced

1 red pepper, cored, deseeded and cut
lengthways into thin strips

1 x 425 g/14 oz can baby sweetcorn, drained

Sauce

3 tablespoons soy sauce

2 tablespoons Chinese wine or dry sherry

1 tablespoon dark soft brown sugar

1 teaspoon five spice powder

heat a wok until hot, add the pepper and dry-fry over a gentle heat for 1–2 minutes. Remove from the wok, crush in a mortar, and set aside.

prepare the sauce: put all the ingredients in a bowl or jug and stir well to mix. Set aside.

heat the wok again until hot. Add 2 tablespoons of the oil and heat over a moderate heat until hot. Add the beef strips, chillies and crushed peppercorns, increase the heat to high and stir-fry for 3–4 minutes or until the beef is browned on all sides. Remove the wok from the heat and tip the beef and its juices into a bowl. Set aside.

return the wok to a moderate heat, add the remaining oil and heat until hot. Add the onion and red pepper and stir-fry for 2–3 minutes or until softened slightly, then add the baby sweetcorn and stir-fry for 1–2 minutes or until hot.

return the beef and its juices to the wok, pour in the sauce and increase the heat to high. Toss for 2–3 minutes or until all the ingredients are combined and piping hot. Serve at once.

Serves 2–3 as a main dish or 4 as part of an Oriental meal
Preparation time: *20–30 minutes*
Cooking time: *9–12 minutes*

clipboard: Szechuan pepper is not, in fact, pepper but is made from the seed casings of a species of prickly ash that grows in the Szechuan province of Western China. Cultivated in the lush, almost tropical climate, it has a superb pungent flavour. It can be bought in Oriental food stores, and is one of the ingredients in Chinese five spice powder.

Roast Beef

with individual Yorkshire puddings

1 roasting joint of beef
Dijon or French mustard
freshly ground black pepper

Yorkshire Pudding
125 g/4 oz plain flour
pinch of salt
1 large egg
300 ml/½ pint milk, or milk and water
margarine or lard for greasing

check the weight of the joint, and calculate cooking time. If the joint has a bone – e.g. rib of beef – allow 1–2 minutes less per 500 g/1 lb. Place the meat in a roasting tin, season with pepper and coat with mustard.

fast-roasting method: preheat the oven to 220°C/425°F/Gas Mark 7. Allow 15 minutes per 500 g/1 lb plus 15 minutes for rare beef; 20 minutes per 500 g/1 lb plus 20 minutes for medium-cooked beef; 25 minutes per 500 g/1 lb plus 25 minutes for well-cooked beef. Reduce the heat to 190°C/375°F/Gas Mark 5 after the first hour's cooking.

slow-roasting method: Preheat the oven to 180°C/350°F/Gas Mark 4. Allow 25 minutes per 500 g/1 lb plus 25 minutes for medium-cooked beef; 35 minutes per 500 g/1 lb plus 35 minutes over for well-cooked beef. Reduce the heat to 160°C/325°F/Gas Mark 3 after 1½ hours. (Slow-roasting is not recommended for cooking rare beef.)

make the Yorkshire puddings: blend the flour, salt, egg and milk or milk and water to make a batter. Whisk just before cooking.

remove the beef from the oven and heat to 230° C/450°F/Gas Mark 8. Grease a deep patty tin, heat well and put in the batter. Cook for 10–12 minutes until well risen. Reduce the oven temperature to the original setting. Return the meat. Continue cooking for 8–15 minutes at the higher temperature or 15–20 minutes at the lower temperature. Remove the meat and pudding. Transfer to a serving dish, and serve with gravy made from the meat juices.

Makes: *12 Yorkshire puddings*
Preparation time: *20–25 minutes*
Cooking time and oven
temperature: *see above*

Beef Tacos

These fried, stuffed tortillas are a favourite fast food in Mexico. They are deservedly popular, and people who like fresh, spicy flavours will find them quite irresistible.

500 g/1 lb steak, minced
75 g/3 oz onion, chopped
65 g/2½ oz green pepper, deseeded and chopped
1 garlic clove, crushed
1 teaspoon dried oregano
½ teaspoon hot paprika
¼ teaspoon ground cumin
¼ teaspoon dried hot red chilli pepper flakes
125 ml/4 fl oz tomato purée
12 tortillas
oil for frying
salt and freshly ground black pepper

To serve
1 lettuce, shredded
2 tomatoes, finely chopped
2 tablespoons Cheddar cheese, grated
1 avocado, diced
150 ml/¼ pint sour cream
Salsa Cruda (see page 9)

cook the minced steak in a frying pan until brown and crumbly, stirring occasionally and breaking it up with a wooden spoon.

add the onion, green pepper and garlic and cook, stirring occasionally, until softened. Stir in the herbs, spices and seasoning to taste.

add the tomato purée and mix well. Cover and cook gently for 10 minutes, stirring occasionally.

place a little of the mixture on each tortilla and roll up. Secure with a cocktail stick and then fry quickly in a little oil until golden. Serve with the various accompaniments.

Serves 4–6
Preparation time: *15 minutes*
Cooking time: *30 minutes*

clipboard: Tortillas are thin pancakes made from unleavened cornmeal. They are now available in larger supermarkets and are sold in packets in ready-to-cook form.

Beef Bourguignon

This is one of the great dishes of French regional cooking, in which the long, slow cooking releases the flavours of the meat, garlic and wine. Use the best Burgundy you can afford, to achieve the most authentic result.

1 large onion, thinly sliced
a few parsley sprigs
a few thyme sprigs
1 bay leaf, crumbled
1 kg/2 lb chuck steak or top rump cut into 2.5 cm/1 inch cubes
2 tablespoons marc or brandy
400 ml/14 fl oz red Burgundy wine
2 tablespoons olive oil
50 g/2 oz butter
150 g/5 oz lean bacon, roughly chopped
24 small pickling onions, peeled
500 g/1 lb button mushrooms, halved
25 g/1 oz plain flour
300 ml/½ pint Beef Stock (see page 10)
1 garlic clove, crushed
1 *bouquet garni*
salt and freshly ground black pepper

put a few onion slices in a deep bowl with a little parsley, thyme and some crumbled bay leaf. Place a few pieces of beef on top and continue layering up in this way until all the onion, beef and herbs are used. Mix together the marc or brandy with the wine and oil and pour over the beef. Cover and leave to marinate for at least 4 hours.

melt the butter in a flameproof casserole, add the bacon and fry over moderate heat until golden brown. Remove and set aside. Add the small onions and fry until golden on all sides. Add the mushrooms and fry, stirring, for 1 minute. Drain and set aside.

remove the beef from the marinade then strain the marinade and set aside. Add the beef to the casserole and fry briskly until browned on all sides. Sprinkle in the flour and cook, stirring, for 1 minute. Gradually stir in the strained marinade then add the stock, garlic and *bouquet garni*. Season to taste, cover and simmer gently for 2 hours.

skim off any fat on the surface, add the bacon, onions and mushrooms to the casserole. Cover and simmer for 30 minutes or until the beef is tender. Discard the *bouquet garni* and serve immediately.

Serves 4–6
Preparation time: *30 minutes, plus 4 hours marinating*
Cooking time: *2½ hours*

Steak, Kidney and Oyster Pudding

Pastry

250 g/8 oz suet, shredded
500 g/1 lb plain flour
50 g/2 oz fresh white breadcrumbs
pinch of salt
300 ml/½ pint cold water

Filling

2 tablespoons plain flour, seasoned
1.5 kg/3 lb rump steak trimmed and cut
into 2.5 cm/1 inch cubes
500 g/1 lb ox kidney, chopped
1 small onion, grated
2 teaspoons Worcestershire sauce
2 teaspoons chopped parsley
6 oysters, fresh or canned
600 ml/1 pint Beef Stock (see page 10)
salt and freshly ground black pepper

grease a 2.3 litre/4 pint pudding basin. Make the pastry: mix together all the dry ingredients then add the water slowly, to make a smooth, pliable dough.

turn on to a floured surface and roll out. Reserve enough to cover the top. Cut a strip long enough to line the basin sides, plus a round for the bottom. Press to seal the edges.

sift the flour on to a flat plate then roll the meat and onion in it and put into the lined basin.

add salt, pepper, Worcestershire sauce, parsley and oysters and mix in carefully. Add the stock, which should not come higher than 2.5 cm/1 inch from the top. Roll out the remaining suet crust to fit the top. Moisten the edge and lay it on, pressing down at the rim.

cover with buttered greaseproof paper or aluminium foil pleated across the middle to allow the pudding to rise. Tie securely and stand in the top of a steamer or else in a deep saucepan.

pour in boiling water. If the pudding is in a saucepan do not let the water come above the rim of the basin. Put the lid on the saucepan or steamer and cook for 4–5 hours, topping up the water as necessary. Longer cooking will only improve the pudding. To serve, remove the paper or foil and wrap the basin in a napkin or folded tea towel.

Serves 6–8
Preparation time: *45 minutes*
Cooking time: *5 hours*

Fillet Steak

baked in pastry

40 g/1½ oz butter
1 tablespoon oil
2 small onions, finely chopped
1 garlic clove, crushed
125 g/4 oz mushrooms, finely chopped
pinch of ground nutmeg
4 fillet steaks, about 175 g/6 oz each, trimmed
250 g/8 oz frozen puff pastry
1 tablespoon plain flour for rolling out
1 egg, beaten
4 slices ham
salt and freshly ground black pepper
fresh chervil or parsley sprigs, to garnish

heat 25 g/1 oz of the butter and the oil in a frying pan and gently cook the onions and garlic until soft. Add the mushrooms, salt, pepper and nutmeg and stir over a gentle heat.

heat the remaining butter in a clean frying pan, add the fillet steaks and then sear quickly on both sides. Remove from the pan, cool quickly and keep chilled until required.

roll out the pastry on a lightly floured surface and cut into 8 rounds large enough to half cover the steaks. Brush a 2.5 cm/1 inch border around the edge of each pastry round with beaten egg. Cut the ham into 8 rounds the same size as the steaks.

place one piece of ham on each of 4 pastry rounds. Cover the ham with a portion of the mushroom mixture, a fillet steak, another portion of mushrooms and another round of ham. Top with a pastry circle. Seal the edges of the pastry between your fingers and then with a fork.

cut any pastry trimmings into leaves and use to decorate. Brush with beaten egg and cook in a preheated oven, 220°C/425°F/Gas Mark 7, for 20 minutes until golden brown. Serve with chervil or parsley sprigs.

Serves 4
Preparation time: *30 minutes*
Cooking time: *30–35 minutes*
Oven temperature: *220°C/425°F/Gas Mark 7*

Fish and Shellfish

Sole Véronique

4 medium sole, skinned and filleted
450 ml/¾ pint water
1 small shallot or onion (optional)
1 parsley sprig
150 ml/¼ pint white wine
125 g/4 oz black or white grapes, skinned and deseeded
salt and freshly ground white pepper

Cream sauce
25 g/1 oz butter
20 g/¾ oz flour
150 ml/¼ pint double cream

To garnish
few extra grapes, deseeded (optional)
fennel or dill leaves

ask the fishmonger for the heads and skins of the fish to make a stock if he prepares the fish for you, or reserve them if you do it yourself. Make a stock: put fish trimmings and water into a saucepan. Peel the shallot or onion but leave it whole and add to the pan with a little seasoning and the parsley. Cover and simmer steadily for 20 minutes. Strain the stock – you need 225 ml/7½ fl oz. Add this to the white wine.

put one or two skinned and deseeded grapes on each fillet of sole before rolling up tightly. Secure the rolls with fine wooden cocktail sticks. Put them into an oblong casserole and cover with the stock; add any remaining skinned and deseeded grapes. Cover and cook in a preheated oven, 200°C/400°F/Gas Mark 6, for 25 minutes or until tender.

lift the fish rolls and grapes from the stock; remove the cocktail sticks from the rolls. Place the fish on a heated dish, cover with kitchen foil so it does not dry and keep hot. Strain and reserve the liquid from the casserole.

make the sauce: heat the butter in a pan, stir in the flour, then blend in 225 ml/7½ fl oz of the reserved liquid. Stir as the sauce thickens, then gradually blend in the cream and any extra seasoning required. Heat gently without boiling, then add the skinned grapes. Spoon the sauce with the grapes on to heated plates. Arrange the fish rolls on top. Garnish with a few extra grapes if liked — deseeded but not skinned — and the fennel or dill leaves. Serve with crisp mangetout and new potatoes.

Serves: 4
Preparation time: *25 minutes (55 minutes if you prepare the fish yourself)*
Cooking time: *50 minutes*
Oven temperature: *200°C/400°F/Gas Mark 6*

clipboard: To skin grapes, place them in a bowl and cover with boiling water. Leave for 1–2 minutes, drain, cut a cross at the stem end of each grape, and peel off the skin.

Classic Fish Pie

1 kg/2 lb potatoes, peeled and cut into chunks
750 g/1½ lb cod, hake or haddock, skinned, filleted
and cut into 4 equal pieces
900 ml/1½ pints milk
75 g/3 oz butter
40 g/1½ oz plain flour
salt and freshly ground black pepper
1 tablespoon chopped chives, to garnish

boil the potatoes in a large saucepan of salted water for about 15–20 minutes or until tender.

arrange the pieces of fish in a dish in 2 layers while the potatoes are cooking. Season with salt and pepper and pour over 750 ml/1¼ pints of the milk. Cover closely with kitchen foil and bake in a preheated oven at 180°C/350°F/Gas Mark 4 for 25 minutes.

drain the potatoes and pass them through a mouli légumes or sieve. Add 40 g/1½ oz of the butter and 150 ml/¼ pint of the milk and beat until soft and creamy. Set aside to cool but do not chill.

melt 25 g/1 oz of the butter in a medium saucepan just before removing the fish from the oven, sprinkle in the flour and cook, stirring, for 1–2 minutes. Remove from the heat. Strain the cooking liquid from the fish and gradually stir into the butter and flour mixture. Return to the heat and cook, stirring, for 2–3 minutes. Season to taste.

pour the sauce evenly over the fish and leave to cool completely.

spoon the potato over the fish, lightly smooth the surface then mark the top in a pattern with a fork. Dot with the remaining butter. Bake on the top shelf of the preheated oven, 180°C/350°F/Gas Mark 4, for about 25 minutes until the fish is heated through and the topping is browned. Serve garnished with the chopped chives.

Serves: 4
Preparation time: *15 minutes, plus cooling*
Cooking time: *50 minutes*
Oven temperature: *180°C/350°F/Gas Mark 4*

clipboard: For a richer pie, stir 2 tablespoons of double cream into the sauce just before pouring it over the fish.

Bouillabaisse

This sumptuous fish stew from the south of France is generally recognized as having originated in Marseilles, though various recipes can be found throughout Provence.

200 ml/⅓ pint olive oil
2 onions, thinly sliced
2 leeks, trimmed and thinly sliced
3 tomatoes, skinned (see page 20), deseeded and chopped
4 garlic cloves, crushed
1 fennel sprig
1 thyme sprig
1 bay leaf
1 strip orange rind without pith
750 g/1½ lb shellfish e.g. crab, mussels, king prawns
2 litres/3½ pints boiling water
2.5 kg/5 lb mixed fish e.g. John Dory, monkfish, sea bass, skinned and filleted
4 pinches of saffron powder
salt and freshly ground black pepper

To serve
slices of hot toast made from French bread
250 ml/8 fl oz Rouille (see page 8)

heat the olive oil in a large saucepan, add the onions, leeks, chopped tomatoes and garlic and sauté over low heat for a few minutes until soft, stirring frequently. Stir in the fennel, thyme, bay leaf and orange rind.

add the shellfish, boiling water and some salt and freshly ground black pepper to the pan. Turn up the heat and boil for about 3 minutes to allow the oil and water to amalgamate.

add whatever fish you are using to the saucepan and reduce the heat. Continue cooking the fish over medium heat for 12–15 minutes until cooked. The flesh should be opaque and tender but still firm – it should not be falling apart.

taste the bouillabaisse when the fish is cooked, and adjust the seasoning. Stir in the saffron, then pour into a warmed tureen or soup dishes.

serve immediately with slices of hot toasted French bread topped with a spoonful of rouille.

Serves: 6–8
Preparation time: *20 minutes*
Cooking time: *30 minutes*

Red Snapper
with limes and coriander

*The fresh, tangy taste of limes and coriander gives
an exciting, aromatic New World flavouring to fish
cooked in this exuberant Mexican style.*

I kg/2 lb red snapper or other white fish,
skinned and filleted

4 tablespoons lime or lemon juice

2 teaspoons salt

4 tablespoons olive oil

25 g/I oz fresh breadcrumbs

I garlic clove, crushed

6 tablespoons finely chopped coriander leaves

I teaspoon grated lime or lemon rind

freshly ground black pepper

warmed tortillas, to serve (optional)

rinse the fish fillets under running cold water and pat dry with
absorbent kitchen paper. Rub the fish with half of the lime or lemon juice
and 1 teaspoon of the salt, and place skin side down in a lightly oiled,
heavy-bottomed frying pan.

add enough cold water to cover the fish and then simmer gently over
low heat for 5 minutes, turning twice during the cooking time.

heat half of the olive oil in another pan, and add the breadcrumbs,
garlic, the remaining salt and 4 tablespoons of the coriander. Cook over
low heat, stirring constantly, until the crumbs are golden brown. Spread
over the fish and simmer for 7–10 minutes until the fish flakes easily.

blend the remaining lime or lemon juice and oil together and pour over
the fish. Cook for 2–3 minutes. Combine the remaining coriander with the
grated lime or lemon rind and sprinkle over the fish. Season with black
pepper and serve hot with warmed tortillas if you want an authentic
Mexican touch.

Serves: 4
Preparation time: *10 minutes*
Cooking time: *20 minutes*

Spicy Fish Stew
with peppers, limes and chillies

3 tablespoons olive oil

1 large onion, chopped

2 garlic cloves, crushed

1 large red pepper, deseeded and chopped

1 large yellow pepper, deseeded and chopped

500 g/1 lb tomatoes, skinned (see page 20) and chopped

2 tablespoons finely chopped fresh root ginger

1 tablespoon chopped fresh coriander

2 teaspoons chopped oregano

rind of 1 lime, grated

few drops of hot chilli sauce

2–4 dried red chillies, chopped

1.2 kg/2½ lb monkfish, skinned, boned and cut into chunks

300 ml/½ pint Fish Stock (see page 10)

12 fresh scallops, cleaned and halved

250 g/8 oz prawns, uncooked

salt and freshly ground black pepper

a few coriander leaves, torn, to garnish

heat the oil in a large, heavy-based saucepan and gently sauté the onion, garlic and the red and yellow peppers for about 10–15 minutes until they are tender.

add the tomatoes, ginger, chopped coriander, oregano, lime rind, chilli sauce and dried red chillies.

stir well to mix thoroughly and then simmer the mixture gently over low heat for 10 minutes.

add the monkfish and fish stock to the saucepan and bring to the boil. Reduce the heat and then simmer gently for 20 minutes.

stir in the scallops and prawns and cook gently for 2 more minutes until they are cooked.

season to taste with salt and pepper and serve the fish stew garnished with torn coriander leaves.

Serves: 6
Preparation time: *15 minutes*
Cooking time: *45 minutes*

clipboard: Scallops are usually sold opened and cleaned. To prepare them yourself, wash them in plenty of water. Open them by placing under a hot grill for 2–3 minutes, then insert a knife between the scallop and the half-shell to which it clings, and free the scallop. Remove the fringe area, and black intestinal thread. Retain only the white cushion and coral, and wash thoroughly.

Baked Sea Bream

with tarragon and lemon

Although there are so many delicious kinds of fish to sample from the fishmongers, most people remain faithful to their old favourites. The flavour of sea bream will be a delightful surprise if you have never tasted it before.

1 x 1–1.25 kg/2–2½ lb sea bream, cleaned and scaled

1 onion, sliced

25 g/1 oz butter

3 small tomatoes, halved

2 tablespoons Fish Stock (see page 10)

100 ml/3½ fl oz water

juice of 1 lemon

1 tablespoon fresh white breadcrumbs

1 tablespoon chopped tarragon

3 tablespoons olive oil

To garnish

1 lemon, halved

tarragon sprigs

place the fish in an ovenproof dish.

fry the onion gently in the butter over low heat for about 15 minutes or until soft and golden brown.

arrange the fried onion and halved tomatoes around the fish and then cover with the fish stock, water and lemon juice.

sprinkle the breadcrumbs, chopped tarragon and olive oil over the dish and then bake in a preheated oven, 180°C/350°F/Gas Mark 4, for 40–45 minutes, basting occasionally. Serve garnished with lemon and tarragon.

Serves: 6
Preparation time: *25 minutes*
Cooking time: *40–45 minutes*
Oven temperature: *180°C/350°F/Gas Mark 4*

clipboard: There are various kinds of sea bream available. This recipe uses the gilt-headed bream or *daurade,* which is its French name. Ask your fishmonger if you are unsure. Sea bream is delicious and comparatively inexpensive.

Fresh Tuna *baked with tomatoes, peppers and garlic*

1 kg/2 lb fresh tuna steaks, 2 cm/¾ inch thick
plain flour for dusting steaks
6 tablespoons olive oil
1 red pepper
1 green pepper
2 onions, sliced
2 large tomatoes, quartered
1 garlic clove, crushed
1 *bouquet garni*
200 ml/7 fl oz dry white wine
salt and freshly ground black pepper
2 tablespoons finely chopped basil to garnish

dust the tuna steaks with seasoned plain flour, then fry them gently in half of the olive oil over low heat, turning once to cook both sides. Remove from the pan and transfer them to an ovenproof dish.

place the red and green peppers under a hot grill in the meantime, turning occasionally until they are charred and blistered all over. Allow them to cool and then skin and slice the peppers, discarding the seeds.

fry the onions gently in the remaining olive oil until soft and golden brown. Add the peppers, tomatoes, garlic and *bouquet garni*.

season to taste and then simmer gently for 20 minutes. Add the wine and bring to the boil. Remove from the heat.

cover the tuna steaks with the sauce and then bake in a preheated oven, 200°C/400°F/Gas Mark 6, for 20 minutes.

reduce the oven temperature to 160°C/325°F/Gas Mark 3, cover the dish and cook the tuna for a further 30 minutes. Serve sprinkled with chopped basil.

Serves: 4–6
Preparation time: *30 minutes*
Cooking time: *50 minutes*
Oven temperature: *200°C/400°F/Gas Mark 6,*
then *160°C/325°F/Gas Mark 3*

Grey Mullet
with red wine and garlic

The flesh of grey mullet has a lovely flavour, and it is a fish that is worth buying when you see it at the fishmonger. Braised in red wine, it is scrumptious.

4 medium grey mullet or whiting, filleted
flour, for coating
75 ml/3 fl oz olive oil
3 tablespoons capers

Red wine sauce
2 tablespoons olive oil
2 onions, chopped
3 garlic cloves, crushed
2 tablespoons flour
500 ml/17 fl oz red wine
250 g/8 oz tomatoes, skinned (see page 20) and roughly chopped
2 tablespoons tomato purée
I *bouquet garni*
salt and freshly ground black pepper

To garnish
2 tablespoons chopped parsley

make the sauce: heat the olive oil in a large saucepan and sauté the onions and garlic until soft and golden. Stir in the flour and cook gently for 1 minute, then add the red wine, stirring well. Bring to the boil.

add the tomatoes to the pan with the tomato purée, *bouquet garni* and seasoning, and then cook briskly, uncovered, for about 30 minutes or until the sauce is thick and reduced.

dust the fish fillets with flour in the meantime. Heat the olive oil in a large frying pan and cook the fish for 3–4 minutes each side, until they are cooked and golden. Remove from the pan, drain and keep warm.

pass the sauce through a sieve, or purée in a food processor or blender. Return to the pan and add the fish fillets. Heat through gently for 5–10 minutes. Add the capers and serve sprinkled with chopped parsley.

Serves: 4
Preparation time: *15 minutes*
Cooking time: *50–55 minutes*

Baked Monkfish

with green pepper sauce

1.25 kg/2½ lb monkfish tail,
skinned and filleted
1 teaspoon dried thyme
2 garlic cloves, cut into thin slivers
juice of ½ lemon
200 ml/7 fl oz dry white vermouth
salt and freshly ground black pepper
2 tablespoons chopped parsley, to garnish

Pepper sauce

3 tablespoons olive oil
2 green peppers, deseeded and chopped
2 onions, finely chopped
3 courgettes, chopped
salt and freshly ground black pepper

season the monkfish fillets with salt and pepper and sprinkle one of them with thyme. Make small incisions in the flesh with a sharp knife and carefully insert the slivers of garlic.

sprinkle with lemon juice and place the other fillet on top of the garlic-studded fillet. Secure with string. Place in an oiled ovenproof dish and add the vermouth. Cover with kitchen foil and bake in a preheated oven, 190°C/375°F/Gas Mark 5, for 30 minutes. Remove the fish and keep warm, reserving the cooking liquid.

make the sauce meanwhile: heat the olive oil in a heavy pan and fry the peppers for about 5 minutes, until softened. Add the onions, courgettes and seasoning and cook very gently, stirring occasionally, for 15 minutes.

add the reserved cooking liquid from the fish to the sauce and boil up for a few minutes, stirring well. Pour the sauce into a baking dish and place the fish on top. Return the baking dish to the oven for 15 minutes, or until the fish is cooked. Remove the string and serve hot, sprinkled with chopped parsley.

Serves: 4–6
Preparation time: *15 minutes*
Cooking time: *45 minutes*
Oven temperature: *190°C/375°F/Gas Mark 5*

clipboard: Monkfish (or anglerfish) has a superb flavour and texture, somewhat similar to that of lobster. It has become very popular and is now widely available at fishmongers and from the fresh fish counters at large supermarkets. It is quite expensive but well worth the money.

Seafood Brochettes *marinated in fresh lime juice*

juice of 2 limes
2 tablespoons olive oil
2 garlic cloves, crushed
500 g/1 lb mixed seafood – e.g. uncooked prawns, fresh tuna, scallops
50 g/2 oz butter, softened
2 hot chillies, chopped (preferably jalapeño)
salt and freshly ground black pepper
few coriander leaves, torn, to garnish

To serve

plain boiled rice

make the marinade: put the squeezed juice of 2 limes with the olive oil and garlic in a large bowl. Mix thoroughly to blend and add some salt and pepper. Put the prepared seafood in the marinade (cut the scallops in half if they are very large) and stir gently until completely coated. Cover and refrigerate for at least 1 hour.

remove the seafood from the marinade and thread alternately on to wooden or metal skewers. Place them on the rack of a grill pan and brush with the remaining marinade. Grill, turning occasionally. until cooked and tender, about 5 minutes. Baste with more marinade if necessary.

make the chilli butter: blend the softened butter with the chopped chillies until they are thoroughly mixed. Arrange the seafood brochettes on 4 serving plates on a bed of rice and put a pat of chilli butter on top of each one. Scatter with torn coriander leaves.

Serves: 4
Preparation time: *20 minutes, plus 1 hour marinating*
Cooking time: *5 minutes*

clipboard: Hot chillies are the most fiery variety of pepper. The intensity of their heat increases as the chilli pepper matures, and can range from mild to scorching hot. Jalapeño chillies come from the Veracruz region of eastern Mexico.

Garlic Prawns
with chillies and limes

4 king prawns, uncooked
6 garlic cloves, peeled
2 red chillies, deseeded and chopped
3 tablespoons olive oil
50 g/2 oz butter
juice of 2 limes
½ teaspoon sea salt
½ teaspoon whole black peppercorns
3 tablespoons chopped coriander, to garnish

To serve
lime wedges
1 avocado, sliced

split the prawns carefully down the middle towards the tail end, without completely separating them. They should look rather similar to butterflies. Remove the dark vein running along the back of each prawn.

crush the garlic cloves with the sea salt, peppercorns and the chopped chillies using a pestle and mortar until you have a thick aromatic paste.

coat the prepared prawns with this garlic mixture and place them in a bowl. Scrape out any remaining garlic paste and spread over the prawns. Cover the bowl and leave in a cool place to marinate for at least 1 hour.

heat the olive oil and butter in a large, heavy-based frying pan and add the prawns and garlic paste. Quickly sauté them over medium heat for 2–3 minutes until they turn pink.

remove from the pan and keep warm. Add the lime juice to the pan and stir into the pan juices.

boil vigorously for a couple of minutes, then pour over the prawns. Garnish with coriander and serve with lime wedges, and avocado slices.

Serves: 4–6
Preparation time: *15 minutes, plus 1 hour marinating*
Cooking time: *5 minutes*

Grilled Seafood Shells

with garlic and mushrooms

600 ml/1 pint mussels, washed and scrubbed
175 g/6 oz queen scallops, cleaned and prepared
50 g/2 oz butter
1 tablespoon onion, finely chopped
1 garlic clove, crushed
50 g/2 oz button mushrooms, sliced
50 g/2 oz fresh white breadcrumbs
150 ml/¼ pint dry white wine
1 tablespoon lemon juice
1 tablespoon chopped parsley
salt and freshly ground black pepper

place the washed and scrubbed mussels in an ovenproof dish with a little water. Put in a preheated oven, 180 C°/350° F/Gas Mark 4, until they open. Remove the mussels from the shells, and separate the white and coral parts of the scallops.

melt half of the butter in a frying pan and sauté the onion, garlic and mushrooms until they are lightly coloured. Mix in the mussels and scallops and heat through gently.

butter 4 deep scallop shells and sprinkle in half of the breadcrumbs. Divide the seafood mixture between the shells. Boil 4 tablespoons of water with the wine and lemon juice until reduced and spoon over the shells.

combine the remaining breadcrumbs with the chopped parsley and seasoning and scatter over the shells. Melt the remaining butter and pour over the top. Place the shells on a baking tray and bake in a preheated oven, 180°C/350°F/Gas Mark 4, for 15 minutes until golden brown.

Serves: 4
Preparation time: *30 minutes*
Cooking time: *15 minutes*
Oven temperature: *180°C/350°F/Gas Mark 4*

Moules Marinière

mussels in wine and garlic

The all-time classic recipe for mussels, this has lots of delicious, fragrant sauce with a wonderful, aromatic flavour. Mop it up with plenty of French bread.

60 g/2½ oz butter
4 shallots, finely chopped
1 garlic clove, crushed
350 ml/12 fl oz dry white wine
1 *bouquet garni*
2 litres/3½ pints fresh mussels, washed and scrubbed
2 tablespoons chopped parsley
salt and freshly ground black pepper
French bread, to serve

melt the butter in a large saucepan, stir in the shallots and garlic and fry gently until soft. Stir in the wine, add the *bouquet garni* and bring to the boil. Boil for 2 minutes, add a pinch of salt and some black pepper to taste, and then add the mussels.

cover the pan and cook over high heat, shaking vigorously from time to time, until the mussel shells open. Remove from the pan with a slotted spoon and set aside. Discard any mussels that do not open.

boil the liquid rapidly until reduced by half, then return the mussels to the pan and heat through for 1 minute, shaking the pan constantly.

sprinkle with the parsley and shake the pan again. Pile the mussels up in a deep warmed serving dish or in individual dishes and pour the liquid over the top. Serve immediately with crusty French bread.

Serves: 4–6
Preparation time: *10–15 minutes*
Cooking time: *20 minutes*

Baked Scallops
with butter and breadcrumbs

This is the simplest method of cooking scallops, and relies completely on the freshness and purity of the fish. Use only the finest scallops for this recipe.

8–10 scallops with their shells, washed and prepared
125 g/4 oz butter
4 tablespoons fresh breadcrumbs
salt and freshly ground black pepper
2 tablespoons chopped parsley, to garnish

reserve the rounded part of 4 shells and chop the white flesh of the scallops coarsely, leaving the orange coral whole.

divide the chopped scallops and coral evenly between the 4 shells and season to taste. Dot the scallops with 50 g/2 oz butter.

sprinkle the fresh breadcrumbs equally between the shells and use the remaining butter to dot over the tops.

cook in the middle of a preheated oven, 180°C/350°F/Gas Mark 4, for about 30 minutes, or until the top is crisp and bubbly and the scallops are thoroughly cooked.

serve immediately, sprinkled with the fresh parsley.

Serves: 4
Preparation time: *30 minutes*
Cooking time: *30 minutes*
Oven temperature: *180°C/350°F/Gas Mark 4*

clipboard: The meat of the great scallop, with its pinkish-orange coral, is quite delectable. The smaller scallop is called the queen, and has tender, tasty meat. Both shells of the queen are rounded, while the great scallop has one flat half shell, and one rounded.

Poultry and Game

Roast Chicken

with bread sauce and gravy

1 x 1.5–2 kg/3–4 lb oven-ready chicken with giblets
1 lemon
1 *bouquet garni*
4 tablespoons olive oil
salt and freshly ground black pepper

Bread sauce
600 ml/1 pint milk
1 small onion, grated
pinch of ground cloves
pinch of ground bay leaves
75 g/3 oz fresh white breadcrumbs
25 g/1oz butter
ground nutmeg
salt

Gravy
2 tablespoons plain flour
300 ml/½ pint Chicken Stock (see page 10), or wine
salt and freshly ground black pepper

remove the giblets from the chicken and reserve for the gravy stock.

put the lemon and the *bouquet garni* inside the chicken cavity and truss the chicken securely.

place the chicken in an oiled roasting tin, pour over the olive oil, and sprinkle with salt and pepper to taste.

roast in a preheated, oven, 180°C /350°F/Gas Mark 4, for 1½–1¾ hours or until the chicken is tender.

prepare the bread sauce 15 minutes before the chicken is cooked. Pour the milk into a pan and add the onion, cloves and bay leaves.

heat until the milk has almost reached boiling point. Stir in the breadcrumbs and butter. Remove from the heat and leave for 5 minutes. Add nutmeg and salt to taste.

make the gravy. Remove the chicken from the oven, and place on a serving dish in a warm place. Pour off all but 2 tablespoons of fat from the pan, leaving the residue. Add the flour to the pan, and stir over low heat until it is bubbling and golden. Gradually stir in the chicken stock or wine. Add salt and pepper to taste.

serve the chicken accompanied by the bread sauce and gravy.

Serves 6
Preparation time: *30 minutes*
Cooking time: *1½–1¾ hours*
Oven temperature: *180°C/350°F/Gas Mark 4*

Tequila Chicken
in pine-nut sauce

The ginger nuts in this unusual Mexican recipe thicken the sauce as well as adding extra flavour.

4 tablespoons sunflower or corn oil
4 chicken portions, preferably leg joints, skinned
2 garlic cloves, chopped
4 medium tomatoes, skinned (see page 20) and chopped
300 ml/½ pint Chicken Stock (see page 10)
few drops Tabasco sauce or a pinch of chilli powder
2 ginger nut biscuits
50 g/2 oz seedless raisins
2 tablespoons tequila or sherry
3 tablespoons pine nuts
salt and freshly ground black pepper

heat 2 tablespoons of the oil in a heavy bottomed frying pan and add the chicken. Cook steadily for 10 minutes, turning over once or twice. Remove from the pan with a perforated spoon. Heat the rest of the oil and add the garlic and tomatoes.

cook for a few minutes. Meanwhile, blend the chicken stock with the Tabasco sauce or chilli powder and pour over the ginger nut biscuits. When these are slightly softened, mash them with the liquid, or sieve, or blend in a liquidizer.

pour this mixture into the pan and stir to blend with the garlic and tomatoes. Add the chicken joints and raisins.

cover the pan and cook for about 10 minutes or until the chicken is tender. Finally, add the tequila or sherry, the pine nuts and any seasoning required. Heat for 2 minutes, then serve.

Serves 4
Preparation time: *30 minutes*
Cooking time: *45 minutes*

clipboard: Pine nuts are now widely available in large supermarkets and give a mild, creamy flavour to foods. Though they are used in many parts of the world, they are most familiar in Italian food – especially as a major ingredient in Pesto sauce.

Turkey and Orange Stir-Fry

with mixed vegetables

Marinade

1 tablespoon soy sauce
2 tablespoons orange juice

Stir-fry

350 g/12 oz turkey breast fillets, skinned
and cut into pieces 4 cm/1½ inch wide and thick
grated rind and juice of 2 oranges
1 tablespoon cornflour
1 tablespoon sunflower oil
1 teaspoon sesame seed oil
½ red pepper, deseeded and cut into neat strips
½ green pepper, deseeded and cut into neat strips
3 celery sticks, diced
125 g/4 oz carrots, peeled and cut
into matchstick slices
salt and freshly ground black pepper

To serve

plain boiled rice

make the marinade: mix the soy sauce and orange juice together. Place the turkey pieces in this and leave for 30 minutes.

measure the orange juice and add sufficient water to give 150 ml/ ¼ pint. Blend the cornflour with this and add a little salt and pepper. Lift the turkey from the marinade and drain well. Save the marinade.

heat the two oils in a wok or heavy frying pan. Add the turkey pieces and stir-fry for 4–5 minutes, then add the orange rind, peppers, celery and carrots. Continue stir-frying for a further 3 minutes.

pour in the cornflour and orange juice mixture, together with any marinade that may be left. Stir as the liquid comes to the boil and thickens slightly.

serve with plain boiled rice.

Serves 4
Preparation time: *25–30 minutes, plus 30 minutes marinating*
Cooking time: *9–10 minutes*

clipboard: Turkey has become very popular as a stir-fry ingredient, as it is tasty and has a good texture. It is now widely available in supermarkets ready-diced for cooking.

Coq au Vin

chicken in red wine

This is one of those recipes that immediately conjures up the essence of French cooking. The classic blend of long-simmered herbs, meat and wine is quite unforgettable.

2 tablespoons oil
50 g/2 oz butter
1 x 2.5 kg/5 lb chicken, cut into 12 serving pieces
24 small pickling onions, peeled
125 g/4 oz smoked bacon, diced
1 tablespoon plain flour
1 bottle good red wine, e.g. Burgundy
1 *bouquet garni*
2 garlic cloves, unpeeled
pinch of sugar
¼ teaspoon freshly grated nutmeg
24 button mushrooms
1 tablespoon brandy
3–4 slices French bread
oil for frying
salt and freshly ground black pepper
a few rosemary sprigs, to garnish
2 tablespoons chopped parsley, to serve

heat the oil and butter in a large flameproof casserole and add the chicken pieces. Fry gently over low heat until golden on all sides, turning occasionally. Remove with a slotted spoon and keep warm. Pour off a little of the fat from the casserole, then add the onions and bacon. Sauté until lightly coloured, then sprinkle in the flour and stir well.

pour in the wine and bring to the boil, stirring. Add the *bouquet garni*, garlic cloves, sugar and nutmeg, and salt and pepper to taste. Return the chicken to the casserole, lower the heat, cover and simmer for 15 minutes.

add the mushrooms and continue cooking gently for a further 45 minutes, or until the chicken is cooked and tender. Remove the chicken with a slotted spoon and arrange the pieces on a warm serving platter. Keep hot. Pour the brandy into the sauce and boil, uncovered, for 5 minutes until thick and reduced. Remove the *bouquet garni* and garlic.

remove the crusts from the bread and cut into pieces. Fry in oil until crisp and golden on both sides. Remove and pat with absorbent kitchen paper. Pour the sauce over the chicken and serve with the bread croûtes. Garnish with the rosemary and serve sprinkled with chopped parsley.

Serves 6–8
Preparation time: *15–20 minutes*
Cooking time: *1½ hours*

Basque-style Chicken *with garlic, ham, tomatoes and peppers*

4 tablespoons olive oil
175 g/6 oz smoked ham or streaky bacon, diced
4 large chicken portions
4 onions, sliced
3 garlic cloves, crushed
2 green peppers, deseeded and diced
¼ teaspoon dried marjoram
425 g/14 oz tomatoes, skinned (see page 20) and chopped *or* 1 x 425 g/14 oz can of tomatoes
150–300 ml/¼–½ pint Chicken Stock (see page 10)
salt and freshly ground black pepper
2 tablespoons chopped parsley, to garnish

heat the olive oil in a sauté pan or deep frying pan. Add the diced ham or bacon and sauté gently, stirring occasionally, until lightly browned. Remove the ham from the pan with a slotted spoon and keep warm.

add the chicken portions to the pan and cook, turning occasionally, until they are uniformly brown. Remove with a slotted spoon and keep warm. Add the onions and garlic and cook gently until soft and golden. Add the peppers and marjoram, cover and cook gently for 10 minutes.

add the tomatoes and some stock (300 ml/½ pint if you are using fresh tomatoes, or 150 ml/¼ pint if you are using canned tomatoes in juice). Season to taste with salt and pepper. Return the chicken and ham to the pan, cover and cook gently for 40–45 minutes, or until the chicken is cooked and tender.

remove the chicken and transfer to a serving dish. Boil the sauce gently to reduce if necessary, until it is thick enough to coat the back of a spoon. Adjust the seasoning and pour over the chicken. Sprinkle with chopped parsley and serve.

Serves 4
Preparation time: *20 minutes*
Cooking time: *1 hour*

Chicken and Olives
with fresh herbs and garlic

175 g/6 oz black olives, pitted and chopped

1 tablespoon chopped parsley

1 tablespoon chopped chervil

1 tablespoon chopped tarragon

1 tablespoon chopped watercress

3 garlic cloves, chopped

150 g/5 oz butter, melted

4 chicken portions

3 tablespoons olive oil

1 *bouquet garni*

salt and freshly ground black pepper

mix half of the black olives with all the fresh herbs, the watercress, garlic and melted butter. Season with salt and pepper.

rub the prepared herb, olive and butter mixture all over the chicken portions, and then transfer them to a large ovenproof dish.

prick the skin of the chicken all over with a sharp knife, and then sprinkle with the olive oil. Add the *bouquet garni* to the dish.

roast the chicken in a preheated oven, 200°C/400°F/Gas Mark 6, for 35–40 minutes.

remove the *bouquet garni* and serve the chicken garnished with the remaining olives.

Serves 4
Preparation time: *10 minutes*
Cooking time: *35–45 minutes*
Oven temperature: *200°C/400°F/Gas Mark 6*

Provençal Chicken
with fragrant herbs

1 x 1.5–2 kg/3–4 lb chicken
juice of 1 lemon
3 tablespoons olive oil
25 g/1 oz butter, melted
pinch of Provençal herbs
1 lemon, peeled and sliced
salt and freshly ground black pepper
lemon slices, to garnish

wash and dry the chicken, place in a roasting tin, and brush it all over with the lemon juice.

mix 2 tablespoons of olive oil with the butter, salt, pepper and herbs. Coat the chicken with this sauce.

place the lemon slices inside the chicken, then roast in a preheated oven, 180°C /350°F/Gas Mark 4, for 1½–1¾ hours.

sprinkle the chicken with the remaining olive oil just before carving.

serve the chicken garnished with lemon slices and accompanied by plain boiled rice or vegetables.

Serves 4
Preparation time: *10 minutes*
Cooking time: *1½–1¾ hours*
Oven temperature: *180°C /350°F/Gas Mark 4*

clipboard: the fragrant wild herbs of Provence are often mixed and dried and then sold in pots as *herbes de Provence*. The ones frequently used are bay, fennel, marjoram, oregano, rosemary and thyme. Use them to flavour meat and vegetable stews, to sprinkle over grilled or barbecued fish, meat and poultry, and to enhance vegetables, soups and gratins.

Burgundy Pheasants

2 plump young pheasants with giblets
small sprig of thyme or pinch dried thyme
50 g/2 oz butter
300 ml/½ pint red Burgundy wine
1 tablespoon arrowroot or cornflour
2 tablespoons redcurrant jelly
2 tablespoons cocktail onions
2 tablespoons stuffed green olives (optional)
salt and freshly ground black pepper

To garnish
redcurrants
parsley sprigs

put the pheasant giblets into a pan with water to cover, add a little salt and pepper and thyme. Cover the pan and simmer for 45 minutes. Strain the liquid and boil briskly until reduced to 300 ml/½ pint stock. If you have no giblets to make stock, use Chicken Stock (see page 10).

put 25 g/1 oz of the butter inside the birds and spread the remainder over the skin. Put them into a roasting tin, and cover lightly with kitchen foil to keep from drying out. Place in a preheated oven, 200°C/400°F/Gas Mark 6, and roast for 40 minutes. Bring the roasting tin out of the oven about 10 minutes before the birds are cooked. Lift them on to a dish and pour out all the fat, straining 1 tablespoon into a pan for the sauce. Replace the birds and pour 3 tablespoons of the wine over them. Return to the oven while you make the sauce.

make the sauce: blend the arrowroot or cornflour with the remaining wine, and add to the fat in the pan with the redcurrant jelly and giblet stock. Stir as the sauce comes to the boil, thickens slightly and the jelly dissolves. Lift the pheasants on to a heated dish. Strain the juices from the roasting tin into the sauce. Boil for a few minutes, then add the well-drained onions and olives, if using, and any extra seasoning required. Heat for 2–3 minutes.

Pour the sauce over the pheasants, and garnish with redcurrants and sprigs of parsley. Serve with accompaniments such as bacon rolls, game chips, fried crumbs, small sausages etc.

Serves 4–6
Preparation time: *20 minutes*
Cooking time: *40 minutes*
Oven temperature: *200°C/400°F/Gas Mark 6*

Duck with Oranges

25 g/1 oz butter

3 tablespoons olive oil

1 x 2 kg/4 lb duck, trussed with thread or string

4 garlic cloves, crushed

125 g/4 oz raw country ham, cut into thin strips

600 ml/1 pint dry white wine

200 ml/7 fl oz Chicken Stock (see page 10)

1 *bouquet garni*

pared rind, and juice of 2 oranges

1 tablespoon wine vinegar

salt and freshly ground black pepper

2 oranges, cut into thin rings, to garnish

Beurre manié

1 tablespoon flour

25 g/1 oz butter, softened

heat the butter and oil in a deep flameproof casserole and add the duck. Fry over medium heat, turning the duck as necessary, until it is golden brown all over.

add the garlic and strips of ham to the casserole and fry for 1–2 minutes. Pour in the white wine and stock, bring to the boil and then simmer for a few minutes until slightly reduced. Add the *bouquet garni*, salt and pepper and orange juice, and then cover the casserole. Reduce the heat and simmer gently for 1½ hours, or until the duck is cooked. Baste occasionally during cooking.

cut the pared orange rind into fine strips with a sharp knife, and plunge them into a small pan of boiling water. Blanch for 5 minutes, then remove and drain. Dry thoroughly on absorbent kitchen paper and set aside.

make the *beurre manié*: blend the flour and butter thoroughly to make a smooth paste. Remove the duck from the casserole, cut into serving pieces and keep warm. Boil the cooking liquid for about 10 minutes, until reduced. Add the vinegar, strips of orange rind and little pieces of *beurre manié*, a few at a time, stirring constantly, until the sauce thickens.

carve and serve with the orange sauce, garnished with orange rings.

Serves 6
Preparation time: *20 minutes*
Cooking time: about *1¾–2 hours*

Game Pie

This is a traditional game pie from East Anglia, which is world famous for its large shoots and excellent game. This pie tastes just as good eaten cold.

25 g/1 oz butter
1 large onion, finely chopped
2 partridges or 1 other small game bird
or 1 pheasant, cleaned and jointed
250 g/8 oz lean steak, cut into 2.5 cm/1 inch pieces
2 rashers bacon, rinded and cut into
1 cm/½ inch strips
125 g/4 oz mushrooms
1 thyme sprig
1 bay leaf
600 ml/1 pint Beef Stock (see page 10)
300 g/10 oz shortcrust or flaky pastry
1 egg, beaten
salt and freshly ground black pepper

melt the butter in a frying pan, add the onion and cook until soft. Add the game joints and brown on all sides. Remove from the pan and reserve. Add the steak and brown lightly.

spread the steak on the bottom of a large pie dish and arrange the game joints on top. Sprinkle the onion, bacon, mushrooms and herbs on top. Season to taste and just cover with stock. Cover with kitchen foil and cook in a preheated oven, 150°C/300°F/Gas Mark 2, for about 1½–2 hours until the meat is tender.

remove the dish from the oven and allow to cool. Increase the oven temperature to 200°C/400°F/Gas Mark 6. Add a little more stock to bring the liquid 1 cm/½ inch from the top of the meat.

roll out the pastry and cut out a lid to fit the dish. Cut a strip 2.5 cm/1 inch wide and lay it around the rim of the dish. Moisten with water, then lay on the pastry lid, pressing it down firmly. Knock back the edges and mark with a knife in ridges. Brush with beaten egg. Roll out the trimmings and use to make leaves or other decorations. Place on the lid and brush with egg again. Return to the oven and bake for 20 minutes.

reduce the oven heat to 150°C/300°F/ Gas Mark 2, place the pie on a lower shelf in the oven and bake for a further 15–20 minutes.

Serves 6
Preparation time: *30 minutes, plus cooling*
Cooking time: *2¼–2¾ hours*
Oven temperature: *150°C/300°F/Gas Mark 2,* then
200°C/400°F/Gas Mark 6, then *150°C/300°F/Gas Mark 2*

Pasta and Rice

Meat-filled Cannelloni

1–2 tablespoons olive oil
375 g/12 oz lean stewing veal, finely diced
1 onion, sliced
1 carrot, sliced
150 ml/5 fl oz dry white wine
300 ml/½ pint Chicken Stock (see page 10)
125 g/4 oz chicken, cooked
125 g/4 oz spinach, cooked and chopped
2–3 tablespoons single cream
12 tubes ready-to-cook cannelloni
2 x quantity Tomato Sauce (see page 8)
40 g/1½ oz Parmesan cheese, grated
salt and freshly ground black pepper

butter an oven-to-table dish and set aside. Heat the oil in a pan and fry the veal until it is golden brown. Remove from the pan, add the vegetables and cook until lightly coloured. Return the veal to the pan with the wine and stock. Season lightly and simmer gently for 40–45 minutes until the meat is tender.

remove the meat and vegetables from the pan and mince or chop finely in a food processor with the chicken. Stir in the chopped spinach. Boil the stock until it has reduced to about 2 tablespoons and stir it into the meat and spinach mixture with sufficient cream to soften the mixture.

pipe or spoon the filling into the cannelloni tubes. Place the filled cannelloni in the oven-to-table dish and pour the tomato sauce over. Bake in a preheated oven, 180°C/350°F/Gas Mark 4, for 40–45 minutes.

sprinkle a little Parmesan over the top 5–10 minutes before the end of the cooking time and serve the rest separately.

Serves 4
Preparation time: *20–30 minutes*
Cooking time: *1–1½ hours*
Oven temperature: *180°C/350°F/Gas Mark 4*

clipboard: To improve the texture of ready-to-cook cannelloni tubes, place them one by one into a dish of boiling water for 1 minute, then drain them well before using. This applies to all ready-to-cook pasta. The simplest way to fill cannelloni tubes is to put the filling mixture into a piping bag, without the nozzle, and squeeze it gently into the tubes.

Spinach Lasagne

baked with cheese sauce

500–750g/1–1½ lb fresh spinach, cleaned and
chopped or 375g/12 oz frozen leaf spinach
1½ tablespoons olive oil
2 onions, finely chopped
2 garlic cloves, finely chopped
10 sheets of ready-to-cook lasagne
salt and freshly ground black pepper

Cheese sauce
50 g/2 oz butter or margarine
50 g/2 oz flour
750 ml/1¼ pints milk
1–2 eggs (optional)
175 g/6 oz Gruyère or Cheddar cheese, grated
2 or 3 tablespoons Parmesan cheese, grated
1 teaspoon English mustard, made up
salt and freshly ground black pepper

cook the fresh spinach in the water left on the leaves after washing; add salt and pepper to taste. Strain thoroughly, then chop finely. Cook frozen spinach as instructed on the packet. Heat the oil, add the onions and garlic and cook until tender. Mix with the spinach.

make the cheese sauce: heat the butter or margarine in a saucepan, stir in the flour, then gradually add the milk. Bring to the boil, then stir or whisk into a smooth sauce.

beat the eggs well, if adding, then whisk into the hot, but not boiling sauce. Do not reheat. Grate the cheese and stir most of it into the sauce, with the mustard and salt and pepper.

place the layers of lasagne, spinach and sauce in an ovenproof dish, beginning with lasagne and ending with lasagne and a coating of sauce.

sprinkle the last of the Gruyère or Cheddar and the Parmesan over the top of the sauce and bake for 25–30 minutes in a preheated oven, 190°C/375°F/Gas Mark 5. Serve hot.

Serves 4
Preparation time: *40 minutes*
Cooking time: *25–30 minutes*
Oven temperature: *190°C/375°F/Gas Mark 5*

Tagliatelle Verde

with bacon, garlic and fennel

6 rashers unsmoked streaky bacon
2 tablespoons olive oil
2 fennel bulbs, finely chopped
2 garlic cloves, finely chopped
4 tablespoons freshly grated Parmesan cheese
300 ml/½ pint fromage frais
3 tablespoons finely chopped parsley
375 g/12 oz spinach tagliatelle (fresh or dried)
salt and freshly ground black pepper
fennel fronds, to garnish

grill the bacon until crisp. Drain on absorbent kitchen paper and set aside. Heat the oil in a pan and add the fennel and garlic.

cover the pan and cook gently over a low heat for 5 minutes until the fennel is just tender.

add the Parmesan, fromage frais and parsley, and season to taste. Simmer over a low heat for 1–2 minutes.

cook the pasta in boiling salted water until *al dente* or just firm to the bite. This will take about 3 minutes for fresh pasta and 10–15 minutes for dried. Drain and toss with the sauce. Transfer to a heated serving dish.

chop the bacon and sprinkle over the pasta. Garnish with fennel fronds and serve at once.

Serves 4–6
Preparation time: *15 minutes*
Cooking time: *15–30 minutes*

clipboard: Green tagliatelle (or tagliatelle verde) is made with spinach – hence the green colour. Spinach is used to make a wide range of green pasta, and looks brilliantly colourful.

Fettuccine *with chilli, prosciutto and tomato sauce*

4 tablespoons olive oil
1 onion, finely chopped
125 g/4 oz prosciutto, diced
2 garlic cloves, crushed
1 fresh chilli, deseeded and finely chopped
750 g/1½ lb tomatoes, skinned (see page 20) and chopped
500 g/1 lb fettuccine or tagliatelle (fresh or dried)
salt and freshly ground black pepper
75 g/3 oz pecorino cheese, freshly grated, to serve

heat the oil in a pan, and gently fry the onion for 3 minutes. Add the prosciutto and cook for a further 2–3 minutes.

add the garlic, chilli and tomatoes, and season to taste with salt and pepper. Cook gently for 10 minutes until thickened.

cook the pasta in boiling salted water until *al dente* or just firm to the bite. This will take about 3 minutes for fresh pasta and 10–15 minutes for dried. Drain and toss with the sauce and grated pecorino.

transfer to a heated serving dish and serve immediately.

Serves 4–6
Preparation time: *15 minutes*
Cooking time: *20–35 minutes*

clipboard: Pecorino Romano is a hard, grating cheese not dissimilar to Parmesan. It has been made for two thousand years in southern Italy. The main ingredient is sheep's milk, and this gives the cheese a very distinctive salty, tangy taste. The name is taken from the word 'pecora' which means ewe. There are several kinds of pecorino, which is generally used like Parmesan.

Oils and Vinegars

Sunflower oil

Pistachio oil

Extra-virgin olive oil

Lemon oil

Corn oil

Sesame oil

Grapeseed oil

Walnut oil

Sesame oil
Sesame oil is extracted from sesame seeds and is used in Oriental cookery to flavour traditional dishes. It is rarely used for frying as it has a low smoking point.

Sunflower oil
High in polyunsaturated fatty acids, it is extracted from sunflower seeds and is used in all cooking methods. It has a light, bland flavour.

Corn oil
This is an extract of maize (corn). It is a light golden and delicately flavoured oil which can be used for frying, salad dressings, mayonnaise and baking. It is high in polyunsaturated fatty acids.

Grapeseed oil
A light, pale green oil extracted from grape seeds, it is used in all methods of cooking, including frying and baking. It imparts very little flavour to foods so is useful when it is essential not to mask the delicate flavours of fish or poultry.

Pistachio oil
A distinctive, fine-quality oil which is expensive to produce and therefore costly to buy, it is used in dressings for its strong nutty flavour.

Walnut oil
An expensive, fine-quality oil made from walnuts, and containing polyunsaturated fatty acids, it has a delicate nutty flavour and is used mainly for salad dressings.

Lemon oil
Lemon oil is used instead of lemon essence, or in light salad dressings. It should be kept in a dark, well-stoppered bottle to preserve flavour.

Extra-virgin olive oil
To be labelled extra virgin, olive oil must be from the first pressing of small, ripe olives and have an acidity of 0.2–1 per cent. Extra-virgin olive oil is expensive and is mostly used in dressings.

Olive oil
A golden green oil with a rich, fruity flavour, this is a blending of oils from second

Balsamic vinegar

Red wine vinegar

Sherry vinegar

Raspberry vinegar

Malt vinegar

Olive oil

White wine vinegar with rosemary

or subsequent pressing, which are then subjected to a process of refinement, with first pressed virgin oils. In Latin countries, olive oil is used for all cooking. It is a good source of mono-unsaturated fatty acids.

Balsamic vinegar

This is the most expensive vinegar available. It is aged in wooden casks for 10–30 years. The finest comes from Modena in northern Italy. It is slightly sweet and is used in dressings and sauces.

Red wine vinegar

This is produced in most of the wine-producing regions of the world and each has its own flavour, depending on the grapes in the region. Chianti vinegar, for example, is made from the light red wines of the Chianti region in Tuscany.

Darker red wine vinegars come from the grape skins being left in the juice.

Sherry vinegar

Rich, mellow sherry vinegar comes from Spain and is distilled in the same manner as sherry. The flavour is very strong, so it is used sparingly in dressings.

Malt vinegar

This is made from malted barley, and originates from northern Europe. It has a very acid flavour and is best used for pickling.

Raspberry vinegar

Raspberry vinegar is made by infusing the flavour of the fruit in white wine vinegar. The vinegar is reduced to burn off the acidity, leaving only the flavour. This is particularly good in salad dressings.

White wine vinegar with rosemary

Herb vinegars like white wine vinegar with rosemary are also made by infusion (see raspberry vinegar). They should be used in dressings where you would use the herb to complement the dish. Basil vinegar, for example, can be used in tomato salads. Tarragon vinegar is delicious with chicken and fish dishes.

Tagliatelle

in smoked salmon and asparagus sauce

375 g/12 oz asparagus
375 g/12 oz tagliatelle or fettuccine (fresh or dried)
125 g/4 oz smoked salmon, cut into thin strips
300 ml/½ pint double cream
1 tablespoon chopped tarragon
salt and freshly ground black pepper
Parmesan shavings, to garnish

cut off the asparagus tips and blanch in boiling salted water for 5 minutes. Use the stems for soup or stock.

drain the tips under cold running water, and pat dry.

cook the pasta in boiling salted water until *al dente* or just firm to the bite. This will take about 3 minutes for fresh pasta and 10–15 minutes for dried pasta.

drain and return to the pan. Toss over a low heat with the asparagus, smoked salmon, cream, tarragon, and salt and pepper, until it is completely heated through.

transfer to a heated serving dish and garnish with wafer-thin shavings of Parmesan.

Serves 4
Preparation time: *10 minutes*
Cooking time: *10–25 minutes*

clipboard: For Smoked Salmon and Mushroom Sauce, use 375 g/12 oz mixed ceps, shiitake, oyster and chestnut mushrooms, instead of the asparagus. Cut into even–sized pieces and stir-fry in 2 tablespoons of olive oil for 5–7 minutes, before adding to the pasta.

Spaghetti

in pepper, aubergine and olive sauce

4 tablespoons olive oil

1 onion, finely chopped

1 x 425 g/14 oz can chopped tomatoes

2 tablespoon tomato purée

150 ml/¼ pint red wine

1 large aubergine, chopped

1 large red pepper, cored, deseeded and finely diced

1 large green pepper, cored, deseeded and finely diced

8 anchovy fillets, drained and chopped

1 garlic clove, crushed

500 g/1 lb spaghetti or linguine (fresh or dried)

75 g/3 oz black olives, pitted

salt and freshly ground black pepper

heat the oil in a pan, and gently fry the onion for 3 minutes.

add the tomatoes, tomato purée, red wine, aubergine, red and green peppers, anchovy fillets and garlic. Simmer gently for 20 minutes.

cook the pasta in boiling salted water until *al dente* or just firm to the bite. This will take about 3 minutes for fresh pasta and 10–15 minutes for dried pasta.

drain and toss with the sauce, adding the olives, and salt and pepper to taste. Serve immediately.

Serves 4–6

Preparation time: *10 minutes*

Cooking time: *23–35 minutes*

Spaghetti

with roasted peppers, coriander and chilli pesto

3 mixed red and yellow peppers
500 g/1 lb spaghetti or fettuccine (fresh or dried)
50 g/2 oz butter, diced

Coriander and chilli pesto
50 g/2 oz fresh coriander, roughly chopped
1 fresh chilli, deseeded and roughly chopped
2 garlic cloves, crushed
2 tablespoons pine nuts
finely grated rind of 1 lime
1 teaspoon salt
8 tablespoons olive oil
50 g/2 oz Parmesan cheese, freshly grated

roast the peppers in a preheated oven, 220°C/425°F/Gas Mark 7, until the skins blacken on all sides.

remove the skins and seeds, then chop the flesh into 1 cm/½ inch dice.

make the coriander and chilli pesto: put the coriander and chilli in a blender or food processor with the garlic, pine nuts, lime rind and salt.

purée until smooth, gradually adding the olive oil. Transfer to a bowl and mix with the Parmesan.

cook the pasta in boiling salted water until *al dente* or just firm to the bite. This will take about 3 minutes for fresh pasta and 10–15 minutes for dried pasta.

drain and toss with the peppers, sauce and butter. Serve immediately.

Serves 6
Preparation time: *20 minutes*
Cooking time: *20–30 minutes*
Oven temperature: *220°C/425°F/Gas Mark 7*

Kedgeree

This is one of the many Anglo-Indian dishes that came from the era of the British Raj. The name derives from the Hindu word khichri (a purée of of rice and lentils, or dhal). The addition of the smoked fish results in a luscious, creamy blend of flavours and textures.

125 g/4 oz long-grain rice
500 g/1 lb smoked haddock
2 eggs
50 g/2 oz butter or margarine
2–3 tablespoons milk or single cream
salt and freshly ground black pepper
chopped parsley, to garnish

cook the rice in boiling salted water for about 12 minutes, or according to the packet instructions, until each grain is dry and fluffy, then set aside.

poach the haddock in a little water for 10 minutes, drain and break the fish into large flakes. Meanwhile, hard-boil the eggs, shell, cut half an egg into wedges for a garnish and chop the rest.

heat the butter or margarine in a large pan, add the fish and the cooked rice and just enough milk or cream to moisten. Heat gently, stirring carefully, so the flakes of fish are not broken. Add the chopped eggs to the mixture and season to taste.

spoon on to a heated dish and top with the parsley and garnish with the egg wedges.

Serves 4
Preparation time: *10 minutes*
Cooking time: *30 minutes*

clipboard: While this is an excellent way of using left-over cooked smoked haddock or other fish, it is so good that it is worthwhile cooking the haddock specially. The fillet is better than a whole fish in this case.

Traditional Paella

Paella is so colourful, fragrant and full of flavour, it is not surprising that it is Spain's most popular dish! It is named after the pan in which it is cooked.

2 tablespoons olive oil
1 small chicken, cut into 8 portions
125 g/4 oz fat pork or bacon, diced
1 large Spanish onion, chopped
2–3 garlic cloves
500 g/1 lb tomatoes, skinned (see page 20) and chopped
1 red pepper cored, deseeded and sliced
250–300 g/8–10 oz arborio rice
600 ml/1 pint boiling water
¼ teaspoon saffron powder or strands
75 g/3 oz chorizo (spicy Spanish sausage), or any spiced sausage thinly sliced
12 mussels on half their shells
12 large prawns, shelled and cleaned
salt and freshly ground black pepper

heat the oil and fry the chicken and pork or bacon until golden and nearly tender. Remove from the pan, add the onion and garlic and cook for 5 minutes or until golden brown.

put in the tomatoes and cook for 2–3 minutes, then add the red pepper and rice.

continue to stir over a gentle heat for 1–2 minutes, mixing the rice with the onion mixture. Boil the water, add the saffron and pour over the rice. Season lightly.

cook steadily until the rice is almost tender. Stir from time to time and make sure that you check the amount of liquid regularly. If necessary, add more boiling water.

return the chicken and pork or bacon to the mixture and continue cooking until almost ready to serve.

add the sausage to the pan with the mussels and prawns and any extra seasoning required. Heat for 5–7 minutes.

serve straight from the paella pan.

Serves 4
Preparation time: *50 minutes*
Cooking time: *35–40 minutes*

Fragrant Rice
with vegetables and cashew nuts

This is a delightfully light and fresh way of cooking rice. It is excellent as part of an Oriental meal, or as a delicious vegetarian dish in its own right.

250 g/8 oz easy-cook long-grain rice
1 cinnamon stick
seeds of 4–6 cardamom pods
3–4 cloves
3 tablespoons vegetable oil
1 green pepper, cored, deseeded and finely chopped
1 onion, finely chopped
1 garlic clove, crushed
125 g/ 4 oz button mushrooms, thinly sliced
125 g/4 oz frozen peas
175 ml/6 fl oz vegetable stock, or water
2 carrots, peeled and grated
100 g/3½ oz cashew nuts
salt and freshly ground black pepper

cook the rice in boiling salted water according to packet instructions, with the cinnamon stick, cardamom seeds and cloves until each grain is dry and fluffy. Drain and set aside, removing the spices.

heat a wok until hot. Add the oil and heat over a moderate heat until hot. Add the green pepper, onion and garlic and stir-fry for 2–3 minutes or until softened slightly.

add the mushrooms and frozen peas, increase the heat to high and stir-fry for 3–4 minutes or until tender.

add the cooked rice and stock or water to the wok and toss to mix with the vegetables, then stir in the grated carrots and about three-quarters of the cashew nuts.

toss for a further minute. Add salt and pepper to taste and serve at once, sprinkled with the remaining cashew nuts.

Serves 4 as an accompaniment
Preparation time: *40 minutes*
Cooking time: *15–20 minutes*

Vegetables

Ratatouille

braised Mediterranean vegetables

Ratatouille is one of those dishes that instantly evokes the spirit of the south of France. The mix of flavours, colours and textures is utterly delicious.

4 tablespoons olive oil
3 onions, finely chopped
3 garlic cloves, finely chopped
750 g/1½ lb tomatoes, skinned (see page 20) and chopped
5 courgettes, sliced
2 large aubergines, sliced
salt and freshly ground black pepper
2 tablespoons chopped parsley

heat the oil and cook the onions and garlic gently for 5 minutes. Add the tomatoes and cook for a few minutes until the juice starts to flow.

add the courgettes and aubergines and stir them all together to mix well. Add a little salt and pepper.

cover the pan and simmer for about 30 minutes, or until the vegetables are softened.

taste and add extra seasoning if necessary, then stir in some of the chopped parsley. Serve with some more parsley sprinkled on the top.

Serves 6–8
Preparation time: *15–20 minutes*
Cooking time: *1 hour*

clipboard: Ratatouille is equally good eaten hot or cold. Make several batches of it in the summer months when there are plentiful supplies of the ingredients available. It freezes well for at least a year, and makes an excellent stand-by dish.

Vegetable Moussaka

50 g/2 oz margarine

3 tablespoons sunflower or corn oil

2 aubergines, thinly sliced

4 potatoes, peeled and thinly sliced

3 large onions, chopped

2 garlic cloves, chopped

3 large tomatoes, skinned (see page 20) and sliced

salt and freshly ground black pepper

Cheese sauce

50 g/2 oz margarine

40 g/1½ oz wholemeal flour

600 ml/1 pint milk

250 g/8 oz Cheddar cheese, grated

½-1 teaspoon mixed spice or grated nutmeg

1 teaspoon French mustard

salt and freshly ground black pepper

1 tablespoon chopped parsley, to garnish (optional)

heat half the margarine and oil in a pan, add the aubergines and potato slices and cook steadily for 10 minutes, turning over once or twice. Remove from the pan.

heat the rest of the margarine and oil, add the onions, garlic and tomatoes and cook for 10 minutes; make sure they do not brown. Mix half the aubergines and potatoes with the tomato mixture and season to taste. Keep the rest of the aubergines and potatoes to make the topping.

make the sauce: heat the margarine, add the flour and stir over the heat for 1–2 minutes, then gradually blend in the milk. Stir until a smooth sauce is formed. Remove from the heat, add approximately 175 g/6 oz of the cheese and season with salt, pepper, mixed spice or nutmeg and mustard.

spoon half of the mixed vegetables into a casserole, add half of the sauce and the remainder of the mixed vegetables. Top with a neat layer of aubergines and potatoes, then the rest of the sauce.

cover the casserole with a lid or foil; make sure this does not touch the sauce. Bake for 1¼ hours in a preheated oven, 160°C/325°F, Gas Mark 3. Remove the lid, add the remaining cheese, return to the oven, raising the heat slightly, and cook for a further 10 minutes, or until the cheese topping has melted. Garnish with chopped parsley, if liked.

Serves 4
Preparation time: *15 minutes*
Cooking time: *about 2 hours*
Oven temperature: *160°C/325°F/Gas Mark 3*

Stuffed Artichokes

4 globe artichokes, cleaned and trimmed

juice of ½ lemon

1 onion, thinly sliced

2 carrots, thinly sliced

1 bay leaf

250 ml/8 fl oz dry white wine

250 ml/8 fl oz water

1 tablespoon arrowroot

salt and freshly ground black pepper

Savoury stuffing

2 tablespoons olive oil

1 onion, finely chopped

2 garlic cloves, crushed

125 g/4 oz raw ham or streaky bacon, chopped

2 tablespoons chopped parsley

50 g/2 oz fresh breadcrumbs

salt and freshly ground black pepper

sprinkle the trimmed artichokes with lemon juice and set aside until you are ready to cook them. Put them in a pan of boiling salted water, simmer for 10–15 minutes and then drain upside-down. Remove the fibrous choke in the centre of each artichoke with a small spoon.

make the stuffing: heat the olive oil in a saucepan and fry the onion and garlic over low heat until soft and golden. Remove from the heat and add the ham or bacon, parsley and breadcrumbs. Stir well and season to taste.

fill the hollow centre of each prepared artichoke with the stuffing mixture. Put the onion and carrots in a flameproof casserole and place the artichokes on top. Add the bay leaf and pour over the wine and water, and add a little salt and pepper. Bring to the boil, then reduce the heat and simmer gently for 45 minutes.

remove the artichokes and keep warm. Strain the cooking liquid into a small saucepan and add the arrowroot which has been dissolved in 3 tablespoons of water. Heat gently, stirring all the time, until the sauce has a creamy consistency. Season to taste and serve hot with the artichokes.

Serves 4
Preparation time: *40 minutes*
Cooking time: *1–1¼ hours*

clipboard: Fresh artichokes have a wonderful flavour, and are easy to prepare for cooking. Remove the stalks and the leaves at the base of each artichoke. Cut off the ends of the leaves. Sprinkle with lemon juice to prevent them discolouring until they are used in the recipe.

Vegetables in Cream Sauce

served on a bed of pasta

125 g/4 oz butter
1 onion, diced
1 carrot, diced
1 celery stalk, diced
125 g/4 oz peas, shelled
2 ripe tomatoes, skinned (see page 20) and chopped
1 large courgette, cut into 1 cm/½ inch cubes
125 g/4 oz thin asparagus stalks chopped
300 ml/½ pint double cream
500 g/1 lb fettuccine or tagliatelle (fresh or dried)
50 g/2 oz Parmesan cheese, freshly grated
2 tablespoons flat-leaf finely chopped parsley
salt and freshly ground black pepper

melt half of the butter, and gently fry the onion, carrot and celery until soft. Add the peas, tomatoes and courgette, and gently fry for 5 minutes.

add the asparagus, and fry for 1 minute. Stir in the cream, and simmer gently until reduced by half. Season to taste.

cook the pasta in boiling, salted, water until *al dente* or just firm to the bite. This will take about 3 minutes for fresh pasta and 10–15 minutes for dried pasta.

drain and toss with the remaining butter, the Parmesan, parsley and half of the sauce.

transfer to a serving dish, spoon the remaining sauce over the top and serve immediately.

Serves 4–6
Preparation time: *15 minutes*
Cooking time: *15–30 minutes*

Mediterranean Vegetables

with fresh herbs

4 tablespoons olive oil
1 garlic clove, crushed
3 large onions, sliced
3 large green peppers, cored, deseeded and sliced
1 x 425 g/14 oz can tomatoes
3 tablespoons chopped parsley or chervil
2 tablespoons chopped basil
2 tablespoons chopped thyme
1–2 tablespoons capers
10–12 black olives, pitted
salt and freshly ground black pepper

heat the oil in a pan, add the garlic and onions and fry very gently for 10 minutes, stirring occasionally.

add the green peppers and cook gently, stirring for 1 minute.

add the tomatoes and their juice, then the herbs and salt and pepper to taste. Bring to the boil, then lower the heat, cover and simmer for 30 minutes, stirring occasionally until the vegetables are very soft. Remove from the heat.

stir in the capers and black olives, then taste and adjust the seasoning. Serve warm, or chilled as a starter.

Serves 4
Preparation time: *20 minutes*
Cooking time: *45 minutes*

clipboard: This is a simple variation of the French vegetable dish ratatouille (see page 154), and may be served chilled in individual serving dishes as a starter. It has a rich flavour, with lots of herbs. Red peppers may be used instead of the green ones suggested here, but they will not give such a good contrast in colour.

Stir-Fried Summer Vegetables

Stir-frying is one of the healthiest ways of preparing food. It is also gratifyingly fast, so you can have delicious garden fresh vegetables from wok to table in minutes!

2 tablespoons vegetable oil

4 spring onions, trimmed and cut into 5 cm/2 inch lengths

2 garlic cloves, thinly sliced

1 cm/½ inch slice root ginger, peeled and shredded

125 g/4 oz French beans, topped, tailed and halved

½ small cauliflower, broken into florets

125 g/4 oz mangetout, topped and tailed

3 celery sticks, sliced diagonally

50 g/2 oz courgettes, sliced diagonally

1 red pepper, cored, deseeded and thinly sliced

1 green pepper, cored, deseeded and thinly sliced

1 yellow pepper, cored, deseeded and thinly sliced

2 tablespoons soy sauce

1 teaspoon sesame seed oil

freshly ground black pepper

heat the oil in a wok or large frying pan, add the spring onions and garlic and stir-fry for 30 seconds without browning.

add all the remaining vegetables, then freshly ground pepper to taste, and toss well. Stir-fry for 2 minutes.

stir in the soy sauce and sesame seed oil and serve immediately.

Serves 6
Preparation time: *35 minutes*
Cooking time: *2–3 minutes*

clipboard: To freeze, transfer the mixture to a rigid container, cool rapidly, then seal, label and freeze for up to 3 months. To cook from the freezer: leave to stand at room temperature for 3–4 hours, then turn into a wok or large frying pan. Pour over the soy sauce and sesame seed oil and stir-fry over brisk heat for 3–4 minutes until the vegetables are hot but still crisp. Serve immediately.

Winter Vegetable Casserole

with cheese topping

2 tablespoons olive oil

3 large onions, quartered

2 garlic cloves, thinly sliced

1 x 425 g/14 oz can tomatoes

150 ml/¼ pint dry white wine

1 small or ½ large celeriac, peeled and diced

4 celery sticks, trimmed and cut into 5 cm/2 inch lengths

6 carrots, quartered

1 green pepper, cored, deseeded and sliced

2 leeks, cut into 5 cm/2 inch lengths

a few cauliflower florets

1 tablespoon tomato purée

2 teaspoons dried mixed herbs

salt and freshly ground black pepper

Cheese topping

175 g/6 oz plain flour

pinch of salt

75 g/3 oz butter

2 tablespoons Parmesan cheese, freshly grated

125 g/4 oz mature Cheddar cheese, grated

2 tablespoons chopped parsley

heat the oil in a large pan, add the onion and garlic and fry gently for 5 minutes without browning, taking care not to break up the onions.

stir in the tomatoes with their juice, and wine, then add the celeriac, celery, carrots and salt and pepper to taste. Cover and simmer for 20 minutes. Stir in the green pepper, leeks, cauliflower, tomato purée and herbs and simmer for a further 10 minutes.

make the cheese topping: sift the flour and salt in a bowl. Rub in the butter until the mixture resembles fine breadcrumbs. Stir in the cheeses and parsley, then sprinkle over the vegetable mixture. Bake the casserole in a preheated oven, 200°C/400°F/Gas Mark 6, for 35–40 minutes, until golden brown. Serve hot.

Serves 4–6
Preparation time: *20 minutes*
Cooking time: *about 1¼ hours*
Oven temperature: *200°C/400°F/Gas Mark 6*

clipboard: To freeze, transfer to a rigid container, leaving 1.5 cm/¾ inch head space. Cool quickly, then seal, and freeze for up to 4 months. To thaw and serve: leave to stand in the container in the refrigerator overnight, or at room temperature for 5 hours, then transfer to a casserole or ovenproof dish.

Vegetables

Cabbage

Broccoli

Corn on
the cob

Leek

Pak choi

Red
onion

Onion

Asparagus

Shallot

Potatoes

Peas

Asparagus
Ensure that the stems are firm and the tips juicy. It is a delicious starter and is also good in sauces and soups.

Broccoli
Related to the cauliflower and cabbage, it is available in late winter and spring.

Cabbage
A highly nutritious vegetable with tightly packed leaves, it can be eaten raw in salads or cooked as an accompanying vegetable. It is available all year round.

Onion
Related to the leek and garlic, the onion can be eaten raw in salads but is more commonly cooked to add flavour.

Red onion
This mild onion is an attractive addition to salads or vegetable dishes.

Shallot
This small, mild onion can be cooked whole in casseroles and is good in delicately flavoured sauces.

Corn on the cob
Also called sweetcorn, it is best in summer and autumn. It is used to make cornflour.

Potatoes
A popular vegetable, they can be cooked in many ways. They first came to England in the 16th century with Sir Francis Drake.

Leek
Mild in flavour, this is excellent in savoury dishes, soups and salads. It has been used as the Welsh national emblem since 640AD.

Peas
Small juicy green seeds encased in a green pod, they can be served as an accompanying vegetable or as part of a casserole.

Carrots
Long root vegetables with

Fennel

Aubergine

Kabocha squash

Carrots

Globe artichokes

Courgettes

Flat mushrooms

Patty pan squash

sweet orange flesh, carrots are highly nutritious, particularly when eaten raw. They can also be cooked in casseroles or served as an accompanying vegetable.

Pak choi
Sometimes called Chinese chard or Chinese white cabbage, it is mild in flavour and can be eaten either raw or braised.

Globe artichokes
These are boiled and the leaves are pulled off one by one and served as a starter with a sauce such as vinaigrette or hollandaise.

Fennel
A bulbous plant with bright green, feathery leaves, this has a slightly aniseed flavour. Both bulb and stalks can be eaten, raw or braised.

Aubergine
Also known as eggplant, this is a fruit but is eaten as a vegetable. It can be boiled, steamed, grilled or sautéed.

Courgettes
Also known as zucchini, it has a delicate flavour, good with meat, fish or poultry. It was raised from seeds brought back by Columbus from the Americas.

Flat mushrooms
Possibly one of the oldest plants in the world, these are available all year round. There are some 250 different types of edible fungus, and flat mushrooms are the largest and have a more developed flavour. They are good in stews, vegetable dishes and soups, and go particularly well with garlic.

Kabocha squash
An edible gourd native to the Americas, it has a mild flavour and can be boiled or steamed and used in soups or stir-fries.

Patty pan squash
An American summer squash with a soft skin, it can be baked or boiled and served with butter. It has a mild flavour.

Rösti Potatoes

Everyone loves this delicious, savoury potato dish. It is warming, simple to prepare, and can be served either as a quick snack or as part of a main meal.

1 kg/2 lb potatoes, peeled and halved
or quartered if large
1 large onion, grated
1 egg, beaten
50 g/2 oz butter
salt and freshly ground black pepper

place the potatoes in a saucepan. Pour over enough water to cover and add salt. Cover, bring to the boil and simmer for 5 minutes. Drain and leave to cool.

grate the potatoes coarsely into a mixing bowl and add the grated onion. Stir in the beaten egg with salt and pepper.

heat the butter in a frying pan and add the potato mixture, spreading it over the pan. Cook over a moderate heat, turning with a spatula when the underside becomes lightly browned (there is no need to turn all the potato at once – just lift one section on to the spatula at a time and turn it over).

cook for about 15 minutes until lightly browned throughout and crisp. Use the spatula to press the potato together to form a large pancake, then cook for 2–3 minutes until the underside is browned and crisp.

turn the pancake over and cook the other side. It is easier to turn over if you invert the pancake on to a plate, then slide the pancake back into the pan to cook the other side.

serve at once, cut into wedges.

Serves 4–6
Preparation time: *10 minutes*
Cooking time: *30 minutes*

Scalloped Potatoes
flavoured with onions

1 kg/2 lb potatoes, peeled and thinly sliced
1 large onion, thinly sliced
150 ml/¼ pint Beef Stock (see page 10)
25 g/1 oz butter, melted
salt and freshly ground black pepper
1 tablespoon chopped parsley, to garnish

make layers of the potatoes and onion in a well-buttered ovenproof dish, seasoning the layers with salt and pepper.

bring the stock to the boil and pour over the potatoes, then brush liberally with the melted butter.

cover with kitchen foil and cook in a preheated oven, 180°C/350°F/Gas Mark 4, for 1½ hours.

remove the kitchen foil and cook for a further 30 minutes or until the potatoes are cooked through and lightly browned.

place under a moderate grill until the potatoes are well browned and crispy on top. Serve hot.

Serves 4–6
Preparation time: *20 minutes*
Cooking time: *about 2 hours*
Oven temperature: *180°C/350°F/Gas Mark 4*

Roast Peppers
in virgin olive oil

4 red, green and yellow peppers
4 tablespoons olive oil
1 tablespoon chopped parsley
2 garlic cloves, crushed or chopped
freshly ground sea salt

place the peppers under a hot grill and cook them until they are black and blistered. Turn them occasionally to cook them evenly on all sides. Place in a polythene bag until they are cool, and then peel away the skins.

cut the peppers open and remove the seeds. Cut the flesh into thin strips and arrange them in a serving dish.

sprinkle with olive oil and scatter with parsley and garlic. Finally, grind a little sea salt over the peppers.

Serves 4–6
Preparation time: *10 minutes*
Cooking time: *15 minutes*

Vegetable Pie
with potato pastry

Pastry

250 g/8 oz self-raising flour
175 g/6 oz butter or soft margarine
1 teaspoon salt
250 g/8 oz cold, cooked mashed potato
1 tablespoon milk
1 egg yolk, beaten

Vegetable filling

250 g/8 oz mixed vegetables, frozen or fresh, diced,
125 g/4 oz mushrooms, sliced
1 large or 2 medium onions, thinly sliced
150 ml/¼ pint Bechamel Sauce (see page 8)
75 g/3 oz Cheddar cheese, grated
salt and freshly ground black pepper

make the pastry: place the flour in a bowl, add the butter or margarine and rub in using your fingertips. Mix in the salt and work the mashed potato into this mixture, adding the milk a little at a time.

knead on a floured board until the dough is smooth and fairly soft. Roll out the pastry and use it to line a large, shallow ovenproof dish. Bake blind (see clipboard) in a preheated oven, 200°C/400°F/Gas Mark 6, for 15 minutes or until it is light golden brown.

cook the mixed vegetables in boiling salted water until just tender and allow to cool. Fry the mushrooms lightly and allow to cool. Fry the onions lightly and allow to cool. Mix the vegetables into the bechamel sauce and season to taste while the pastry is cooking.

remove the pastry from the oven, allow to cool a little and then fill with the vegetable mixture, spreading with a palette knife so that it is smooth and flat. Sprinkle with the grated Cheddar. Brush the edges of the pastry with the beaten egg yolk and return to the oven for 15 minutes or until the cheese is melted and beginning to brown. Serve hot.

Serves 4
Preparation time: *30 minutes, plus cooling*
Cooking time: *30 minutes*
Oven temperature: *200°C/400°F/Gas Mark 6*

clipboard: Baking blind is a method of pre-cooking a pastry base without a filling. After lining the dish with the pastry, prick it all over with a fork. Cut a piece of greaseproof paper to the shape of the dish and about 5 cm/2 inches larger all round, and place it over the pastry. Pour enough dried beans over the paper to cover it, then place in the oven for 15 minutes. Remove from the oven, and remove the paper and beans.

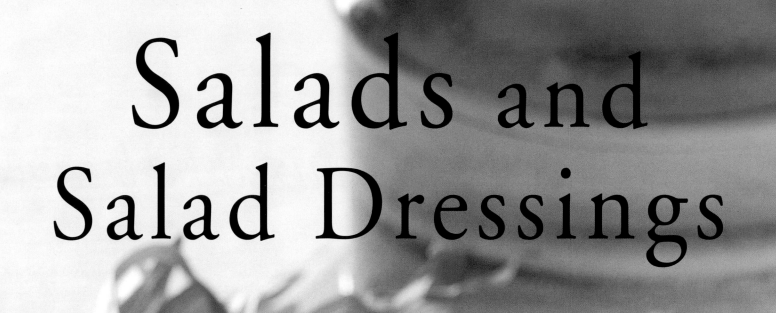

Salads and Salad Dressings

Green Salad

with a mixed herb sauce

1 round lettuce
1 batavia lettuce
125 g/4 oz corn salad

Herb sauce
2 eggs, hard-boiled
2 tablespoons double cream
2 tablespoons olive oil
2 teaspoons white wine vinegar
1 tablespoon chopped chives
1 tablespoon chopped dill
1 tablespoon chopped tarragon
salt and freshly ground black pepper

break the round lettuce leaves in pieces and pile in a salad bowl. Using only the pale green inner leaves of the batavia lettuce, scatter them over the lettuce and put the corn salad on top.

make the herb sauce: separate the whites and yolks of the hard-boiled eggs.

chop the egg whites and scatter over the green salad. Mash the egg yolks to a paste with the cream, and stir in the oil very gradually.

add the vinegar slowly and stir until blended. Add salt and pepper to taste, and stir in the herbs.

pour the herb sauce over the salad and mix well.

Serves 4
Preparation time: *10 minutes*

clipboard: Batavia, also called escarole, is a type of endive. Though it is slightly less curly-leaved than endive, it has a similar, slightly bitter taste which provides an interesting contrast of flavour in green salads.

Spiced Coleslaw
with curry and paprika

Spiced dressing

3 tablespoons Mayonnaise (see page 200)
½ teaspoon curry powder
½ teaspoon ground nutmeg
½ teaspoon paprika
1 teaspoon ready-made English mustard
1 tablespoon olive oil
1 tablespoon lemon juice
salt and freshly ground black pepper

Salad

¼–½ white cabbage or cabbage heart
1 unpeeled dessert apple, cored and diced
2 carrots, grated
2 tablespoons diced gherkins
2 teaspoons capers
2 tablespoons chopped parsley

make the dressing first by blending all the ingredients together. Do this before preparing the salad so it does not become dry.

shred the cabbage finely by hand or with a food processor or blender.

add the apple and carrots to the dressing, together with the gherkins, capers and parsley. Mix together thoroughly.

Serves 4
Preparation time: *25–30 minutes*

clipboard: You should avoid making coleslaw too far ahead, as the cabbage and other ingredients should remain as fresh and crisp as possible. This is a popular salad, and the recipe can be varied in several ways. If you want a lighter dressing, substitute yogurt for the mayonnaise. If you prefer a less spicy option, omit the spices from the dressing. Children often like an extra-crunchy coleslaw, which you can make by adding chopped celery, chopped nuts, more apple and diced, fresh pineapple to the ingredients.

Roast Vegetable Salad

The flavour imparted by roasting gives vegetables a deep, seductive, smoky taste and silky texture. A range of vegetables can be prepared in this way – onions, garlic, peppers, aubergines, courgettes, fennel and artichokes are typical examples.

2 Spanish onions, unpeeled
500 g/1 lb small aubergines
2 sweet red peppers
3 firm but ripe large tomatoes
8 garlic cloves
1 teaspoon cumin seeds
3 tablespoons lemon juice
4 tablespoons virgin olive oil
3 tablespoons white wine vinegar
salt
2 tablespoons finely chopped parsley, or torn basil leaves, to garnish

place the onions on a baking sheet and bake in a preheated oven, 180°C/350°F/Gas Mark 4, for 10 minutes. Add the aubergines and bake for a further 10 minutes. Add the peppers and bake for 10 minutes before adding the tomatoes and 6 of the garlic cloves.

cook for a further 15 minutes, until all the vegetables are tender. If necessary, remove any vegetables that have cooked more quickly than the others. When the vegetables are cool enough to handle, peel them carefully with your fingers.

cut the cores and seeds from the peppers and cut the flesh into strips. Halve the tomatoes, discard the seeds and slice the flesh. Slice the aubergines into strips and the onions into rings. Arrange the peppers, tomatoes, aubergines and onions in a serving dish.

pound the roasted and raw garlic and the cumin seeds to a paste. Use a pestle and mortar or the end of a rolling pin in a small bowl. Gradually beat in the lemon juice, oil and vinegar, then add salt to taste. Pour over the vegetables and sprinkle with parsley or basil. Serve warm or cold.

Serves 4
Preparation time: *5–10 minutes*
Cooking time: *45 minutes*
Oven temperature: *180°C/350°F/Gas Mark 4*

Salade Niçoise

Provençal salad with tuna and anchovies

1 garlic clove, bruised
1 lettuce
125 g/4 oz celery hearts, thinly sliced
125 g/4 oz cucumber, peeled and thinly sliced
250 g/8 oz small French beans, topped and tailed
250 g/8 oz canned artichoke hearts, thinly sliced
500 g/1 lb tomatoes, skinned (see page 20), deseeded and quartered
1 large green pepper, cored, deseeded and sliced
1 onion, sliced
4 eggs, hard-boiled and halved
50 g/2 oz black olives, pitted
8 canned anchovy fillets, drained
1 x 250 g/8 oz can tuna fish in oil, drained

Dressing

7 tablespoons olive oil
4 basil leaves, finely chopped
salt and freshly ground black pepper

rub around the inside of a large salad bowl with the bruised garlic clove. Line the bowl with lettuce leaves.

chop the remaining lettuce leaves roughly and then arrange them in the bottom of the bowl.

mix the celery and cucumber together with the French beans and artichoke hearts. Arrange on top of the lettuce in the salad bowl.

arrange the quartered tomatoes, sliced pepper and onion, eggs, olives and anchovies on top of the mixed vegetables in the bowl.

cut the tuna into chunks and place in the bowl.

make the dressing: mix together the olive oil and chopped basil with salt and pepper to taste.

pour the dressing over the salad and transfer to individual serving plates.

Serves 4
Preparation time: *20 minutes*

Chickpea Salad
with garlic and olives

This is a delicious salad – chick peas are deservedly popular for their mild, creamy flavour, and have a wonderful affinity with olive oil and garlic.

250 g/8 oz chickpeas, dried
1 bay leaf
1 parsley sprig
1 thyme sprig
3 tablespoons olive oil
1 onion, finely chopped
2 garlic cloves, crushed
125 g/4 oz black olives, pitted
½ red onion, finely sliced
salt and freshly ground black pepper
thyme sprigs, to garnish

Vinaigrette dressing
6 tablespoons olive oil
1 tablespoon red wine vinegar
juice of ½ lemon
2 tablespoons chopped fresh herbs, such as parsley
and thyme

put the chickpeas in a bowl, cover with cold water and leave to soak overnight. The following day, drain the chickpeas and rinse thoroughly under cold running water.

put the chickpeas in a saucepan and cover with fresh cold water. Add the bay leaf and sprigs of parsley and thyme.

bring to the boil, and after 10 minutes lower the heat to a bare simmer. Cook gently for about 2 hours, or until the chickpeas are tender.

drain and discard the herbs. Meanwhile, heat the olive oil in a frying pan, and add the onion and garlic.

cook gently over low heat until the onion is softened. Take care that it does not brown.

mix the vinaigrette ingredients together until thoroughly blended. Place in a bowl with the drained chickpeas and sautéed onion.

toss gently while the chickpeas are still hot, and season. Add the olives and red onion and leave to cool. Garnish and serve at room temperature.

Serves 6–8
Preparation time: *15 minutes, plus soaking*
Cooking time: *2¼ hours*

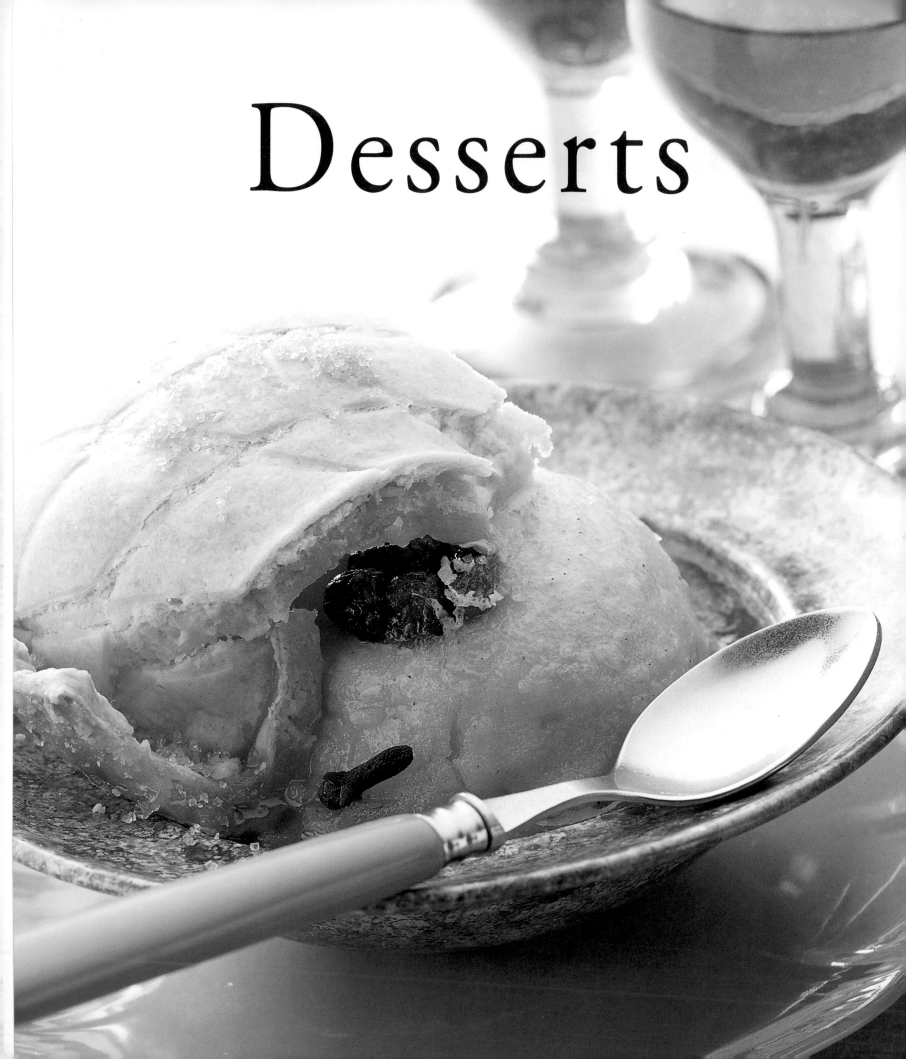

Desserts

Summer Fruit

Granny Smith

Strawberries

Nectarine 'Big John'

Nectarine 'Sunlite'

Golden Delicious

Cox's Orange Pippin

Blackberries

Raspberries

Blueberries

Granny Smith

The Granny Smith was originally an Australian apple. It is both crisp and juicy, and has a bright green skin and particularly sweet-tasting flesh.

Cox's Orange Pippin

This is one of the most popular English apples. It has a fresh-looking green and red skin and a medium soft flesh with a sweet, slightly acid flavour.

Blackberries

These are the small, purplish black, juicy berries of the bramble or blackberry bush. Blackberries are at their best picked fresh in the late summer and early autumn, and are particularly good in jams and pies.

Golden Delicious

This a French apple with soft, pale greenish yellow skin. It has soft flesh and a mild flavour.

Strawberries

Related to the rose, the strawberry bush bears red juicy berries with seed-pitted skin and small green leaves. Strawberries have a delicate, sweet taste. They are delicious served by themselves or with cream, in jams, ice cream, tarts and pies. They also make an attractive garnish. Strawberries are at their best in the summer.

Raspberries

The raspberry is the soft pinkish red fruit of the thorn bush, which is related to the rose. It a delicious fruit, eaten either with cream or ice cream or puréed for use in pies or tarts. Originally from northern Europe, raspberries are available in mid-summer through to the autumn. They freeze well.

Nectarines

Related to the peach, the nectarine has smooth, yellowish red skin and a

Plums

Apricots

Cherries

Pear 'Rocha'

Pear 'Comice'

Redcurrants

sweet golden flesh surrounding a large stone. It can be eaten on its own or used in fruit salad. Two popular varieties of nectarine are 'Big John' and 'Sunlite'. They are at their best in late summer.

Blueberries

A small soft purple-blue berry from North America, the blueberry is sometimes

known as a huckleberry. It has a mild, sweet taste and is good for use in jams, pies or eaten fresh.

Plums

Round, shiny fruit ranging in colour from yellow to purple, plums have sweet flesh with a single flat stone. This variety is the Santa Rose, which is good raw, in a fruit salad, or stewed.

Apricots

The apricot is the same size as the plum but golden in colour with a similar flavour to the peach. It can be eaten raw on its own, or cooked, when it has a tart, tangy flavour and is used in both sweet and savoury dishes.

Redcurrants

They can be eaten fresh, though they are sometimes

tart, and are excellent in jams, sauces and as a garnish.

Cherries

These are small, round, juicy fruits with a single stone, which range from tart to sweet in taste. Available in the early summer months, they can be eaten raw, in pies, in preserves, or with some meat dishes – in particular duck.

Pears

The pear, which originated in Asia, is a yellow, green or brown, soft-skinned fruit. It has juicy, sweet white flesh. It is good eaten by itself, in fruit salad, or poached in syrup or wine. Pears are at their best in early summer to late autumn. Two of the most common varieties are the Comice and the Rocha, shown here.

Fruit Compôte

with summer garden fruits

Nothing is easier to make or more delicious to eat than this simple dessert. It has all the fresh flavours and jewel colours of traditional garden fruits.

500 g/1 lb mixed redcurrants, blackcurrants and blackberries, washed
125 g/ 4 oz caster sugar
250 g/ 8 oz raspberries
whipped cream, to serve

place the currants and blackberries in a heavy pan with the sugar. Cook gently over a low heat, stirring occasionally, for 10 minutes until tender.

remove from the heat, add the raspberries, and set aside to cool.

spoon into individual serving bowls and serve with whipped cream.

Serves 6
Preparation time: *10 minutes, plus cooling*
Cooking time: *10 minutes*

Treacle Pudding
with hot treacle sauce

Treacle pudding is one of the great British traditions, and tastes absolutely wonderful. Steamed to a light, fluffy texture, it readily absorbs the delicious, aromatic sauce.

125 g/4 oz butter or margarine, plus extra for basin
125 g/4 oz caster sugar
2 large eggs
125 g/4 oz self-raising flour, sifted
4 tablespoons golden syrup

Treacle sauce
4 tablespoons golden syrup
1 tablespoon water

butter a 900 ml/1½ pint pudding basin.

cream the butter or margarine and sugar together in a bowl until light and fluffy. Beat in the eggs, 1 at a time, adding a little of the flour with the second egg. Fold in the remaining flour.

spoon 4 tablespoons of golden syrup into the buttered pudding basin, then put the sponge mixture on top.

cover with buttered foil, making a pleat across the centre to allow the pudding to rise. Steam for 1½–2 hours.

make the sauce: heat the syrup and water in a small pan. Turn out the pudding on to a warmed serving dish and pour over the hot sauce just before serving.

Serves 4
Preparation time: *20–30 minutes*
Cooking time: *1½–2 hours*

Coffee and Brandy Ice Cream

3 eggs
75 g/3 oz caster sugar
300 ml/½ pint single cream
3 tablespoons instant coffee powder
300 ml/½ pint double cream
3 tablespoons brandy

beat the eggs and sugar together until smooth. Bring the single cream and coffee just to the boil in a small pan, then stir into the egg mixture.

transfer to the top of a double boiler, or to a heatproof bowl over a pan of simmering water.

cook gently, stirring constantly, until the custard is thick enough to coat the back of a spoon.

strain into a bowl and leave to cool, stirring occasionally to prevent a skin forming.

whip the double cream until it will stand in soft peaks, then fold into the cold custard with the brandy.

pour into a rigid container, cover and freeze for 2–3 hours until half-frozen. Remove from the freezer and stir well, then return to the container.

seal and label, then return to the freezer for up to 3 months. Transfer the ice cream to the refrigerator 30 minutes before serving to allow it to soften.

scoop into chilled glasses or dishes and serve immediately.

Serves 6–8
Preparation time: *20 minutes, plus freezing*

Exotic Fruit

Papaya

Canteloupe melon

Clementine

Mandarin

Water melon

Orange

Mango

Kiwi fruit

Tamarillo

Lychees

Grapes

Water melon
Its sweet, juicy red flesh can be eaten on its own or used in drinks, sorbets or salads.

Lychees
A native of China, lychees have a grape-like flavour and are used in fruit salads and savoury dishes. They are at their best in summer.

Canteloupe melon
Probably the most famous dessert melon, it has sweet, pale orange flesh.

Kiwi fruit
Also known as the Chinese gooseberry, it has sweet, juicy green flesh and black pips. It can be eaten by itself or used in fruit salad or sorbets.

Papaya
Also known as the paw paw, it has orange flesh and dark seeds, in season in summer.

Native to the US, it is eaten by itself or in fruit salad.

Mango
It has sweet golden flesh and a large single seed. In season in summer, it can be eaten by itself or used in curries, chutney or ice cream.

Clementine
Grown mainly in Mediterranean countries, it has sweet juicy flesh and

firm skin. It can be eaten by itself or used in dessert dishes, pickles and vinegars.

Grapes
Grapes can be dried to make currants or sultanas. They are also delicious eaten on their own.

Tamarillo
Native to Peru, this has sharp-tasting flesh, used in sweet and savoury dishes.

Mandarin
Also called a tangerine, it is a small fruit of the orange family, with a loose orange skin and sweet juicy flesh.

Orange
This is the best known of all the citrus fruits and can be eaten either on its own or in fruit salads. Both the juice and the rind can also be used to add flavour to sweet and savoury dishes.

Bananas

Persimmon

Pink grapefruit

Pineapple

Lemon

Custard apple

Grapefruit

Mangosteen

Lime

Pomegranate

Kumquats

Physalis

Kumquats
This tiny citrus fruit, from Brazil, has a sweet-and-sour taste and is eaten unpeeled. It can be candied.

Grapefruit
Larger than the orange and sharper in taste, it has yellow skin. It is eaten by itself, often with sugar.

Pink grapefruit
This grapefruit has pink flesh.

Lime
Its sour juice is used in desserts and savoury dishes. It is refreshing in drinks.

Lemon
Available all year round, its juice and rind are used in sweet and savoury dishes.

Mangosteen
It has soft white flesh similar to that of the lychee. It is eaten by itself.

Persimmon
It has soft, sweet, golden flesh. It can be eaten by itself or in fruit salad. Native to Japan and China, it is in season in the late autumn and early winter.

Physalis
Also known as the cape gooseberry, this is a small orange berry with a papery husk. The fruit is sweet and juicy and is eaten whole.

Custard apple
Originally from Peru, it has juicy white flesh and a sweet and sour flavour with a rose-like scent. The chilled fruit is cut in half, the black seeds are removed, and it is usually eaten with a spoon. It can also be eaten in fruit salads and sorbets.

Pineapple
Its yellow flesh is sweet and juicy and is good on its own

or added to savoury or sweet dishes. It is best in spring.

Banana
It has soft, starchy flesh and can be eaten by itself or used in sweet or savoury dishes.

Pomegranate
The juice is used to make grenadine, and the seeds are used in fruit salad and ice cream. From Asia, it is in season in late autumn.

Raspberry Sorbet

500 g/1 lb raspberries, fresh or frozen
125 g/4 oz sugar
300 ml/½ pint water
2 egg whites

thaw the raspberries at room temperature for 3–4 hours if you are using them from the freezer.

pass the raspberries through a sieve. Put the sugar and water in a saucepan and stir over a gentle heat until the sugar has dissolved.

increase the heat and boil briskly, without stirring, for 8 minutes or until a syrup has formed. Allow to cool.

stir the syrup into the raspberry purée and pour into an ice tray or shallow rigid container.

place in the freezer for 1 hour or until just smooth. Whisk the egg whites until stiff and fold into the raspberry mixture.

return to the container. Cover and seal, then return to the freezer.

to serve: thaw, covered, in the refrigerator for 10–15 minutes, or microwave uncovered on Defrost for 2–3 minutes. stand 3 minutes before serving.

Serves 4–6
Preparation time: *10 minutes, plus freezing*

clipboard: If you have a glut of fresh raspberries from your garden, make this recipe in the summer, and you will have a delicious sorbet available throughout the year at very little cost. For a special occasion, pour a little liqueur, such as Cointreau, over each serving.

Devonshire Splits

Served with clotted cream and jam, these are the basis of the famous Devonshire cream tea. When served with clotted cream and black treacle, they are known as 'Thunder and Lightning'.

15 g/½ oz fresh yeast or 5g/¼ oz dried yeast
½ teaspoon caster sugar
150 ml/¼ pint tepid water
25 g/1 oz lard
50 g/2 oz butter
6 tablespoons milk
500 g/1 lb plain flour
pinch of salt

To serve
icing sugar
clotted cream or whipped cream
jam

sprinkle the fresh yeast and sugar over the tepid water and leave until it is frothy. (If using dried yeast, mix with the sugar and tepid water and leave in a warm place for about 10 minutes, until it becomes frothy.)

put the lard, butter and milk into a small saucepan and heat gently until the fats have melted, but on no account let it boil. Remove from the heat and allow to cool.

meanwhile, sift the flour and salt into a mixing bowl, make a well in the centre and pour in the yeast and milk mixtures, then mix with your fingers until it is soft but not sticky.

turn on to a floured surface and knead gently for 5 minutes, then put into a bowl and leave, covered, in a warm place for 1 hour.

take out and knead again a little, then shape into about 18 small balls. Place them on a greased baking sheet a little apart, and leave until they have spread and are just touching.

bake in preheated oven, 200°C/400°F/Gas Mark 6, for about 20 minutes or until risen. When cooked, they should sound hollow when tapped. Dust with icing sugar, and serve with clotted cream and jam.

Makes about 18 buns
Preparation time: *25 minutes, plus rising*
Cooking time: *20 minutes*
Oven temperature: *200°C/400°F/Gas Mark 6*

Acknowledgments

Special photography by William Adams-Lingwood

All other photos:
Octopus Publishing Group Ltd. / Martin Brigdale, Nick Carman, Jean Cazals, Laurie Evans, Graham Kirk, Sandra Lane, Diana Miller, Peter Myers, Roger Stowell, Paul Williams, Trevor Wood.

Home economist
Bridget Sargeson

Acknowledgments

Special photography by William Adams-Lingwood

All other photos:
Octopus Publishing Group Ltd. / Martin Brigdale, Nick Carman, Jean Cazals, Laurie Evans, Graham Kirk, Sandra Lane, Diana Miller, Peter Myers, Roger Stowell, Paul Williams, Trevor Wood.

Home economist
Bridget Sargeson